Nonprint in the Elementary Curriculum

NONPRINT
IN THE
ELEMENTARY CURRICULUM

Readings for Reference

Edited with an introduction by
James L. Thomas

1982

**Libraries Unlimited, Inc.
Littleton, Colorado**

LIBRARIES UNLIMITED, INC.
P.O. Box 263
Littleton, Colorado 80160

Library of Congress Cataloging in Publication Data

Main entry under title:

Nonprint in the elementary curriculum.

    Bibliography: p. 103
    1. Audio-visual education. 2. Education,
Elementary-- Curricula.   I. Thomas, James L.,
1945-
LB1043.N66   372.13'3   81-15672
ISBN 0-87287-273-4   AACR2

TABLE OF CONTENTS

INTRODUCTION

Educators have maintained and research has shown that individual differences among students require that teachers use a variety of media to reach the intellectual abilities of learners.[1] If we accept these findings, then it becomes clear how essential it is that all media be made available to students in the learning process.

Those of us who have had direct contact with the student of the 70s have at times perhaps been baffled, amazed, or possibly frustrated with conventional instructional approaches that for some reason did not elicit the response we have been taught to expect. As educators we have been ill-prepared to meet the needs of students who have been bombarded and overcharged with the electronic media. John Culkin, in examining this new breed of student, states that "The learner these days comes to school with a vast reservoir of vicarious experiences and loosely related facts; he is accustomed to communication through image and sound; he wants to be involved in what he is doing; he wants to use all his senses in his learning as an active agent in the process of discovery. A new learner calls for a new kind of learning."[2] If we are to reach this "new learner," then we must be willing to utilize all formats to enable our young people to discover and develop the tools necessary for survival in the 80s.

Although nonprint media is still considered by some only to supplement a print-oriented/printed-dominated curriculum, more and more educators are experiencing the value of using other modes of communication to tap the individual styles of each learner. Morrow, Suid, and Suid in "Uncommon Sensing: A Model for Multi-Media Learning" have explored the design of "wheel learning," an approach that divides classroom learning into eight progressive, overlapping areas from awareness of the body to speech to design to print to photography to sound to movies to television. In their research they maintain that "Time and again, we have seen students who bring a long tradition of personal failure with print into the classroom begin to learn in a multimedia situation."[3] One of the main values they see with using such an approach is that "When a child can see print as just one member of the media family, he tends to view it more as a potential tool for communication than as a hurdle."[4]

The purpose of this particular compilation is to document the variety of ways *nonprint*, multimedia experiences have been used in the elementary setting. In reviewing the literature over the past ten years it became evident that nonprint has become more of an accepted and integral part of the school curriculum. It has been used by teachers and school library media specialists to enhance, to motivate, and to increase interest in learning across a variety of subjects. Numerous programs have also been developed in the study of nonprint in its own right, such as production of materials by students and/or visual literacy programs.

In *Nonprint in the Elementary Curriculum*, the editor has selected articles that are representative of the wide variety of ways nonprint materials have been applied to the curriculum; no other compilation to date has taken such an approach. Textbooks that have promoted the utilization, production, and study of nonprint have typically discussed each individual medium and then have attempted to show how each might apply to or be used in instruction.

This particular work includes articles written by practitioners over the past ten years and is divided into the following areas: language arts and reading; mathematics and science; art and music; production of materials in the media center and classroom; and visual literacy programs. Although the articles in the compilation are divided into specific areas, it is hoped that the reader will be able to see applications of the use or production of nonprint across the curriculum, and, as a result, be able either to replicate or to adapt the technique to his or her own subject field. Each section is preceded with a brief overview of the individual articles. An annotated bibliography for additional reading and appendices conclude the collection.

Although this compilation is a retrospective view of the last decade, most of the techniques for using and producing nonprint are still valuable and are worth emulating. Admittedly, as newer methods develop and as educational technology expands, some of these techniques will change or be replaced. However, it should be evident even to the casual reader that the widespread increase of nonprint in the curriculum during the 70s might serve as a predictor for its continued growth and acceptance during the 80s as a viable means for actively involving our young people in their own education process.

—James L. Thomas

NOTES

[1]William H. Allen, "Intellectual Abilities and Instructional Media." *AV Communication Review* (Summer 1975):139-70.

[2]John Culkin, "Education in a Post-Literate World." In *The Mediate Teacher: Seminal Essays on Creative Teaching*, selected and introduced by Frank McLaughlin. Philadelphia, PA: North American Publishing Company, 1975. p. 17.

[3]James Morrow, Murray Suid, and Roberta Suid, "Uncommon Sensing: A Model for Multi-Media Learning." In *The Mediate Teacher: Seminal Essays on Creative Teaching*. p. 36.

[4]Ibid., pp. 36-37.

CONTRIBUTORS

CARLOTTA BOGART is a teacher with the Nashville Davidson County Public School in Tennessee. "What You See's Not All You Get" by Annelle S. Houk and Carlotta Bogart is reprinted from *Elementary English* (March 1974, vol. 51, pp. 445-48). Copyright © 1974 by the National Council of Teachers of English. Reprinted by permission of the publisher and the authors.

ANDD WARD CIPRIANO, Ph.D., is a director of television commercials and motion pictures with D.A.C. Productions. "Student-produced Media through Organized Chaos" is reprinted from *Audiovisual Instruction* (October 1974, vol. 19, pp. 16, 18). Reprinted by permission of the Association for Educational Communications and Technology, 1126 Sixteenth Street, NW, Washington, DC 20036.

DR. CAROLE COX is an associate professor in the Department of Curriculum and Instruction, College of Education, Louisiana State University, Baton Rouge. "The Liveliest Art and Reading" is reprinted from *Language Arts* (September 1975, vol. 52, pp. 771-75, 807). Copyright © 1975 by the National Council of Teachers of English. Reprinted by permission of the publisher and the author.

HETTY CRAMER is an elementary grade teacher. "Super Cinderella—Fourth Graders Put Fantasy on Film" is reprinted by permission of *Audiovisual Instruction* (March 1976, vol. 21, pp. 70-71) and the Association for Educational Communications and Technology, 1126 Sixteenth Street, NW, Washington, DC 20036.

BONNIE DALZELL is a freelance writer who now resides in Glenside, Pennsylvania. "Exit Dick and Jane?" is reprinted from *American Education* (July 1976, vol. 12, pp. 9-13) courtesy of the U.S. Department of Education.

DOROTHY DUTTON, Ed.D., is a remedial reading specialist with the Gunnison Watershed School District in Colorado. "I'm My Own Teacher Aide!" is reprinted from *Instructor* (February 1974, vol. 83, p. 126). Copyright © 1974 by the Instructor Publications, Inc. Used by permission.

NANCY EARLE is the illustrator for "Little Red Riding Hood" originally published in the *Journal of Reading* (November 1974, pp. 106-13). Reprinted by permission of the International Reading Association.

ROY FERGUSON is English chairperson at Milford High School in Ohio. "Seeing Sequentially: A Curriculum" is reprinted from *Audiovisual Instruction*

(May 1972, vol. 17, pp. 16-18). Reprinted by permission of the Association for Educational Communications and Technology, 1126 Sixteenth Street, NW, Washington, DC 20036.

ROBERT T. GASCHE is Coordinator of Instructional Media, P. K. Yonge Laboratory School, College of Education, University of Florida in Gainesville. "Yes, They Can Make Slides, Use a Dry Mount Press, and More" is reprinted from *Audiovisual Instruction* (March 1976, vol. 21, pp. 60-61). Reprinted by permission of the Association for Educational Communications and Technology, 1126 Sixteenth Street, NW, Washington, DC 20036.

ROBERT H. GOLDSMITH is a professor at Saint Mary's College of Maryland. "Personal Inquiry Slides" is reprinted by permission of *Science and Children* (April 1972, vol. 9, p. 20), copyright © 1972.

DR. M. JEAN GREENLAW is an associate professor at the College of Education, North Texas State University, Denton. "Visual Literacy and Reading Instruction: From Books to Media and Back to Books" is reprinted from *Language Arts* (October 1976, vol. 53, pp. 786-90). Copyright © 1976 by the National Council of Teachers of English. Reprinted by permission.

ANNELLE S. HOUK is an educational consultant in Mount Juliet, Tennessee. "What You See's Not All You Get" by Annelle S. Houk and Carlotta Bogart is reprinted from *Elementary English* (March 1974, vol. 51, pp. 445-48). Copyright © 1974 by the National Council of Teachers of English. Reprinted by permission of the publisher and the authors.

DR. ALAN J. McCORMACK is professor of zoology and science education at the University of Wyoming at Laramie. "Wonderblob and the Idea Machines" is reprinted from *Instructor* (January 1979, vol. 88, pp. 111-12, 14, 16). Copyright © 1979 by The Instructor Publications, Inc. Used by permission.

LOLA J. MAY is a math consultant for the Winnetka Public Schools in Illinois. "Teaching Tools: How to Use Them in Math" is reprinted from *Grade Teacher* (February 1970, vol. 87, pp. 126-28, 130). Copyright © 1970 by Macmillan Professional Magazines. Used by permission of The Instructor Publications, Inc.

ANNE D. MODUGNO is chairwoman of the music department at Greenwich High School in Connecticut and is instructor and director of the Electronic Music Lab at the University of Bridgeport. "Electronic Creativity in the Elementary Classroom" is reprinted by permission of *Today's Education* (March 1971, vol. 60, pp. 62-64).

ED PRICE is a former audiovisual consultant for the Garrett County Maryland Board of Education in Oakland, Maryland. "Filmmaking in the Classroom: Scratching on Film" is reprinted from *Teacher* (May/June 1974, vol. 91, pp. 30-31). Copyright © 1974 by Macmillan Professional Magazines. Used by permission of The Instructor Publications, Inc.

MARY LOU RAY is Director of Learning Services for KRMA television station in Denver, Colorado. "Videotaping: You and Your Kids Can Do It" is reprinted from *Teacher* (January 1975, vol. 92, pp. 47-48, 106). Copyright ©

1975 by Macmillan Professional Magazines. Used by permission of The Instructor Publications, Inc.

JULIUS F. SCHILLINGER is director of media services for Lake Erie College in Painesville, Ohio. "Science through Photography" is reprinted by permission of *Science and Children* (September 1973, vol. 11, pp. 33-35), copyright © 1973. "Media Are Tools for Children" is reprinted from *Audiovisual Instruction* (March 1976, vol. 21, pp. 67-69). Reprinted by permission of the Association for Educational Communications and Technology, 1126 Sixteenth Street, NW, Washington, DC 20036.

LISA M. SPAZIANI is an elementary school teacher in Pennsylvania. "Using Student-produced Videotapes for Language Arts and Career Education Programs in the Elementary School" is reprinted from *Audiovisual Instruction* (October 1974, vol. 19, pp. 20-21). Reprinted by permission of the Association for Educational Communications and Technology, 1126 Sixteenth Street, NW, Washington, DC 20036.

BETTY J. SWYERS is an instructor in the area of children's materials with Virginia Commonwealth University and a freelance writer. "Slide into Art" is reprinted from *Grade Teacher* (October 1971, vol. 89, pp. 30-31, 34). Copyright © 1971 by Macmillan Professional Magazines. Used by permission of The Instructor Publications, Inc.

ROY E. TOOTHAKER, Ed.D., is presently an elementary school teacher in the public schools of Kansas City, Missouri. He is the author of numerous professional articles and has published a children's book with Prentice-Hall entitled *A Wild Goose Chase*. "Fostering Visual Literacy: A Fun Exercise" is reprinted from *Arts and Activities* (June 1979, vol. 85, pp. 52-54, 65).

ELISE WENDEL is a library media specialist at the Orchard Road School in Skillman, New Jersey. "Starting Out in Media Production" was originally published in *School Library Journal* (November 1979, vol. 26, p. 49) and is reprinted by permission of the author. *School Library Journal* is published by R. R. Bowker (a Xerox Company). Copyright © 1979 by Xerox Corporation.

MARY HELEN YOUNGS is a former supervisor of audiovisual services and materials with the Fairfax County Public Schools in Virginia. "8mm in the Science Program" is reprinted from *Instructor* (January 1970, vol. 79, p. 102). Copyright © 1970 by The Instructor Publications, Inc. Used by permission.

I

LANGUAGE ARTS AND READING

The language arts and reading areas probably receive more instructional attention than any other area in the elementary curriculum. Educators see the development of communication skills as essential for the child to function eventually in an adult world. Although most teachers of elementary children still use print as the main resource for instructing in language and reading proficiency, the attainment of these abilities depends heavily on the individual child's interest and readiness. As revealed in the articles included for this section, some educators have found that the use of nonprint to motivate and reinforce print increases the likelihood of success.

Carole Cox shows how the use of film production in the classroom may be a motivator for children to read with a purpose. As the child reads, he or she is gathering information with the intent of sharing visually with others. Lisa M. Spaziani, in designing a language arts curriculum, saw that a primary need of her students was the development of oral communication skills. Instead of using filmmaking, she chose the videotape format for on-location interviewing by her students of a variety of professionals. Not only were her students learning to develop questioning skills, but they also found themselves discovering many new career options not previously recognized.

Bonnie Dalzell records in "Exit Dick and Jane?" how a teacher of academically weak students used regular television scripts with the accompanying video as a motivational tool to help poor readers. This was the first time that many of these students had ever experienced the connection between the printed page and the television they had watched at home.

The final article in this section by Dorothy Dutton gives a variety of reasons for using the tape recorder in a listening center for individual and group reading activities. The author maintains that pre-readiness skills as well as post-activity skills are appropriate uses of such centers. Also, while she is working with one group in a live situation, she has extended her capabilities by prerecording activities for others to develop listening and comprehension skills.

THE LIVELIEST ART AND READING   Carole Cox

Film, the liveliest art, can be an integral part of any classroom teacher's reading program. Film and reading are both communication skills and may be woven together in many ways: for motivation, vocabulary growth, comprehension, and critical reading skills, reading for purpose and meaning, extending reading, reading as a thinking process, and creative reading to name a few. Here are several suggestions for ways that teachers can relate filmmaking activities to reading.

Children's literature is one rich source of film plots, narratives, characterizations, settings, images, and moods. Granting that the modern film is a unique art form and more than just a visual interpretation of the written word, it can still draw strength from related arts like literature and illustration. No art is produced in a vacuum, and ideas from children's literature can merge with the child's own experience to create a particular vision of the world through moving pictures. Film can motivate children to read with a purpose, and as George Spache has said: "Students who can set strong purposes for their reading comprehend significantly better than those who set vague purposes."[1] What stronger purpose for reading might be set for today's media-oriented children than searching for ideas that will set a new film rolling in their minds?

Creative filmmaking meshes particularly well with the individualized approach to reading because the children select their own reading materials. The films they make can embody ideas and images from the books they have read. Then, filmmaking becomes a unique way of sharing these books, an activity widely encouraged by educators such as Helen Darrow:

> "Sharing activities provides individuals with a sense of satisfaction
> in progress and accomplishments, motivating them toward greater
> achievement. Group members benefit by getting valuable infor-
> mation; sharing leads to new reading and insights into the many pur-
> poses and pleasures of reading,"[2]

Reviewing books with suggestions for filmmaking possibilities, or preparing a list or card file of these books (or other books on photography and filmmaking) are two activities to interest others in reading. The making of the film itself, be it fanciful or documentary, is an excellent activity to share feelings and impressions, and to extend learnings. As the audience, the rest of the class participates in the sharing by becoming critical viewers and potential film reviewers.

Children's literature and trade books are not the only printed source of ideas for films. Newspapers, comics, and books in the content areas such as social studies and science can inspire filmmaking. Children can easily be encouraged to keep a sharp eye out for anything that might give them an idea for a film. For

Reprinted by permission of *Language Arts* 52 (September 1975):771-75, 807.

example, two films I have made with children were in large part motivated by books and other reading materials. One film drew ideas from a children's literary classic, the other from a science program on the behavior of mealworms. Both groups of children were experienced in creative dramatics and playwriting, and had discussed the possibilities of filmmaking with me. They were looking for ideas to film, and looked as they read.

Magic Matches

Ten children in grades 3-6 borrowed several ideas from C. S. Lewis', *The Lion, The Witch, And The Wardrobe* (1950), and translated them into cinematic images. The children conceived a film that moved from reality to fantasy. In finished form, it included a quest for treasure, a fight against evil, wicked creatures bent on the children's destruction, benign creatures aiding the beleagured children, and a magic device to wisk them away from their homes to ... The North Kingdom! Their film was not merely a literal rendering of *The Lion, The Witch, And The Wardrobe.* The children invented their own characters, story and magic land (North Kingdom). Still, their inspiration remained Lewis' plot, setting and characters. Just as fine painting and music have so often served as stimuli for the creative mind of the writer, so can good literature provide raw material for the imaginative filmmaker. Nature, life and the other arts serve as the basic stuff from which the creative mind observes, selects, and rearranges something new and beautiful. As a part of our humanistic tradition, children's literature can provide endless ideas for the child filmmaker to filter through his or her creative consciousness and recreate in visual form.

I Love You, Mealworm

After experimenting with live mealworms, reading about their behavior in science books, and writing creative "mealworm" stories, my third and fourth grade class decided to use these activities as a springboard for filmmaking. Their film took a "Laugh-In" quickie format—each child had a minute or two of his/her ideas on film. Many of these sequences stimulated extensive reading with a purpose. Some alluded to literature or history, e.g. "The Midnight Ride of Tenebrio Militar," "Wormeo and Julieworm," "Swiss Family Wormison," and "Superworm." Others required research to gain technical knowledge of animation methods, drawing on a film, fast and slow motion techniques. In short, reading material for this film ranged from charts graphing the amount of bran a mealworm consumes in one day to Shakespeare, comics, to technical data on film animation. The children read widely for a specific purpose and did extensive silent reading with attention to meaning. Their reading became what Russell G. Stauffer terms, "the reading-learning-living process."[3]

In addition to reading for a purpose, what other part does reading play in all this cinematic activity? What kinds of reading skills and competencies are needed and developed during filmmaking? Preparing a workable shooting script (essential to even the most sophisticated filmmaker) encourages learning skills related to reading. For instance, script preparation makes the child practice the skill of ordering, which educators agree is important to reading. Filmmakers often use a special story board form for blocking out a film's visuals and sounds (children relish using these special papers to organize their ideas preparatory to using the camera.) They are sheets with four large squares to frame scenes in a vertical column on the left hand side. The right hand side of the page allows for comments, dialogue, shooting directions and sound effects. The complexity of the film requires organization, prethought, ORDERING. The future success of the film depends on it, and it is my experience that the child will do almost anything to make his/her film succeed. Hence, script-preparation has application and meaning. It is a reading and language skill in use, not merely reading and language usage.

Communication is another important educational reward coming from script preparation. Children working in a group must effectively communicate and cooperate in order to construct a workable script, and the individual child must materialize the images and ideas into script form so that others involved in the film — cameramen, actors, etc. — can read and carry out the ideas in the film. All this is in keeping with Jean Piaget's belief that social interaction or sharing is crucial in a teaching-learning experience. Children need to share their ideas and learn from each other, says Piaget. They need to realize that there are more ways of doing things than the single one they thought of.

As a result, they should develop critical thinking.

> The mere fact, then, of telling one's thought, of telling it to others, or of keeping silence and telling it only to oneself must be of enormous importance to the fundamental structure and functioning of thought in general, and of child logic in particular.[4]

Stauffer, proponent of the language experience approach to reading, puts it another way, and explains the implications of communication to reading:

> The bond between word and action and thought, between language and experience, between reading and writing and communication, is of enormous importance. What educationally significant conclusions can we draw from these facts? It would seem that the most functional way to show children that reading is no more than speech written down is to do a great deal more than we do about using their language-experience-cognitive wealth to share each other's intellectual life.[5]

Besides giving practice in the vital learning aspects of ordering and communication, scripts also provide practice in other critical reading skills. If children are filming a story they have read, it is absolutely essential that they be able to outline the plot, much as they would for a story dramatization for creative drama. And they do not need to be told to do an outline. They soon realize that the creation of a film demands it. Scripts often require that the child be able to create, use, and read symbols, which are frequently used as shooting directions, i.e. symbols indicate panning from left to right, a close up or dolly shot, etc. In this respect, the child-filmmaker must be able to interrelate visuals (sketches of scenes in the story board frame), symbols (shooting directions), and words (dialogue or director's notes). They must effectively encode and decode symbols when using a script. They must critically read, interpret and apply what they have read to the production of the film.

After a period of motivation, reading, script development, collection or creation of sets and costumes (which can also demand purposeful reading, say for the purpose of building a "correct" space ship), children move onto the climactic period of filmmaking, The Shooting. Shooting means cameras, film lights and action — a great deal of action, both in front and behind the camera. Again, the link to reading is not broken. The activity, language, and the ideas of a child have a close relationship during the actual shooting of the film. If the children are dramatizing a story they have read, they are trying to be, really be, the characters they have read about. Or they are trying to capture a mood, image, or setting on film if a book is the source of their ideas. Some educators believe that reading and language are directed most effectively when they are used in action. Jerome Bruner argues that when language conveys the content of experience, there is,

> " ... more often than not a requirement of developing cor-
> respondence between what we do, what we see, and what we say. It is
> this correspondence that is most strikingly involved in reading and
> writing, in school learning, and in other abstract pursuits."[6]

If this is true, then filming and role playing are ideal ways for children to employ language and reading actively, and to make reading and language live. George Spache calls this kind of activity "active reacting to reading"[7] and maintains that it is a key aspect of good reading comprehension. It is my belief that there are few activities elementary children would find more interesting, stimulating, or active than filmmaking.

While several reading skills are in use throughout the entire filmmaking process, many of them come into play most actively during the shooting of the film. For instance, a child acting the part of a story character is strongly "identifying with story characters," and "identifying and evaluating character traits." Moreover, it is seldom that only the child actually performing the role benefits from the activity. The remainder of the class should get involved. They form their own ideas about the film characters, consider the director's and actor's interpretation, form their own opinions about characterization, and offer suggestions for change. Or they may simply reinforce what they regard to be a flawless film. In any case, the filmmaker's classmates become critics. No idle hands or thoughts are allowed on the set!

Once characters have been developed, the group must then address itself to "perceiving relationships," and "recognizing emotional reactions and motives" among characters in the story. Some lively discussion can emerge through use of these skills, as in the case of my third and fourth graders who filmed an "epic poem" they had written. This was the tale of Prince Herbie, a noble mealworm of royal connections, who was captured, imprisoned, and finally released from his pet store jailers by a teacher who purchased him for class study. "Seeing" the poem on film prompted a heated class discussion about the wisdom of the classroom teacher, e.g. was she really a hero for "freeing" the mealworm only to put the creature into another confining setting (classroom laboratory)? By itself, the poem had not elicited such sophisticated thinking, and it became necessary after the viewing of the mealworm film to reread the poem, refilm the sequence, and discuss both to satisfy everyone that the author's intentions had been respected, and the teacher's character faithfully portrayed.

In addition to "using imagination," "forming sensory impressions," and "reacting to mood or tone," the child-filmmaker must constantly "visualize characters, settings and events" while reading. If the students have been motivated by the prospect of making films during the school year, they may plot out characters and settings throughout their reading experiences; or at least while practicing other critical reading skills related to filmmaking such as "research" or "obtaining ideas from many sources."

Relating story experiences to personal experiences occurs in the filmmaking process just as it does in reading, creative writing and other language activities. In planning and shooting a film, the child draws on personal experiences, just as the writer does. He or she may take ideas from books, or other printed sources, but the end product is more than visual literary interpretation. All his/her experiences lead the filmmaker from a kind of imaginative Gestalt to the final visual product.

Aside from its many language skill benefits, filmmaking deserves more attention in the classroom for the excitement it stirs in today's media-centered students. Turning a camera on turns children on. No one will look out the window when you are choosing a camera operator, no one will moan when you pass out paper to write a shooting script or story board ideas, and no one will complain about the responsibility and extra effort of "starring" in a film. Filmmaking offers a new kind of creative freedom to the child. It defies a structured approach. It thrives equally as an individual creative effort and a collaborative group endeavor. Films are hard work, but it is my experience that children are willing and eager to perform all kinds of exasperating tasks in order to make a film. They will spend hours hashing out ideas, reading for background information, making properties, setting up scenes, writing and rewriting, shooting and reshooting, and editing (the most exasperating task of all). Despite these demands filmmaking excites children. One of the students said it better than I can:

> Film is expression, a feeling, communication, life that is recorded.
> Film is art. It is a lot to edit. Film is work. Film is fun.

Not through any fault of their own, elementary school teachers have seldom recognized the language value of filmmaking in the classroom.[8] Filmmaking's kinship to reading is too little acknowledged. Films can be one-child or multi-children projects, and thus can tie in to both individualized and group reading approaches. In search of movie plots, moods, settings, characters, and costume ideas, the young filmmaker may comb classic children's literature; or may find them in comic books and other common reading fare. Science books may spark film ideas. Wherever students find ideas, the search will have them reading with a purpose. Making films also gives children practice in those skills useful to good reading. They must learn to order their ideas, to plan or outline the various steps of the film. Research habits are developed. Devising and manipulating symbols is crucial. Communication between the filmmaker, "crew and cast," and other classmates acting as critics is one of the most important benefits of filmmaking. Allied goals such as perceiving relationships, recognizing emotional reactions and motives, and relating story experiences to personal experiences can all be achieved in the classroom filmmaking process. Film is art. Film is language and film is fun. If success in learning to read is in some measure dependent on the child's language life, then filmmaking is a natural asset to the reading program. Young filmmakers use language in a variety of ways: talking over images and ideas for films, preparing scripts, rewriting, shooting and editing.

Jeannette Veatch suggests that:

> ... those activities that enhance a child's ability to use words freely, spontaneously, and communicatively will improve reading at surprising rates. These are better reading activities than those traditionally labeled as such, as they are vital and dynamic in character.[9]

There are few activities one can name that are more vital or dynamic than film-making. Films even move.

References

1. George Spache, *Reading in the Elementary School* (Allyn, 1969), p. 467.

2. Helen Darrow and Virgil Homes, *Approaches to Individualized Reading* (Appleton, 1960), p. 54.

3. Russell G. Stauffer, *The Language Experience Approach to Reading* (Harper, 1970), p. 124.

4. Jean Piaget, *The Language and Thought of the Child* (Humanities Press, New York, 1965), p. 64.

5. Russell Stauffer, *The Language Experience Approach to Reading*, p. 16.

6. Jerome Burner, *Studies in Cognitive Growth* (Wiley, 1966), p. 322.

7. George Spache, *Reading in the Elementary School*, p. 454.

8. Film has not been a part of the traditional curriculum until recent years when the interest of children and teachers in the mass media and the availability of inexpensive equipment, such as Super 8, have encouraged the growth of screen education in the elementary school.

9. Jeannette Veatch, *Reading in the Elementary School*, 1966, p. 357.

USING STUDENT-PRODUCED VIDEOTAPES
FOR LANGUAGE ARTS AND
CAREER EDUCATION PROGRAMS IN
THE ELEMENTARY SCHOOLS

Lisa M. Spaziani

What can you say about a group of children who are eager to communicate? In a modernized world with computer printed travel information, self-service gasoline plazas, and automatic highway toll plazas, our society is becoming one of few words.

After teaching fifth grade for one year, I found a need for methods to enhance oral communication skills. Children "free-talk" very well among peers, yet when placed in a situation where they have to communicate with adults they are generally at a loss for words. This is particularly true in cases where the topic of conversation is one with which they are not familiar. In planning a language arts curriculum for the following school year, I decided to devote a considerable amount of time to communication—specifically oral communication. I developed a curriculum to include such topics as conversation, discussion, debate, panel discussions, oral reports, dramatics, story-telling, and interviewing.

To start the children into the curriculum, we worked on a conversation and discussion unit wherein much time was spent conversing and deliberately discussing topics in which the children indicated an interest. Discussion is a form of oral communication that lends itself well to the study of interviewing techniques, and that is how it was used. As children learn to discuss topics which are both familiar and unfamiliar to them, they find the need (and the ability) to question and seek information. Questioning to seek specific information and listening to receive and use that information are two very important aspects of the interviewing technique.

The interviewing unit proved to be one that the children, school district, and community will be a long time forgetting. It aroused unbelievable enthusiasm and excitement on the part of the children because it was such a unique experience, and on the part of the adults involved because the children were carrying it out.

To begin the unit we discussed the term interview, defined it, watched professional interviews, and dug right in. The children were asked to suggest township and public servants that they might be interested in interviewing. It should be noted that their reaction at this point was one of excitement over the novelty and anxiety over the task of carrying on an interview with such persons as a state policeman, a state representative, a judge, an attorney, a jail warden, and the school district superintendent. The prospect of interviewing important figures was frightening indeed. Once we overcame the authority gaps, we were ready to discuss questioning techniques.

Reprinted by permission of the author and the Association for Educational Communications and Technology from *Audiovisual Instruction* 19 (October 1974):20-21.

We used our prospective subjects and their professions as points of reference. In class groups we worked on possible questions to pose to the interview subjects. Questions covered such areas as: duties, initial interest in their professions, education required, and division of labor.

One might question the reasons for using people outside of the school environment as interview subjects. Children become familiar with their daily environment as well as with school personnel, and naturally speak more freely to those with whom they are acquainted. Moreover, the children were compelled to conduct interviews on subjects with which they had little previous experience and knowledge.

Our next effort was eliciting the services of our district media specialist, without whose help the program would never have gotten off the ground. Our district has the good fortune of possessing videotape equipment. In order to evaluate the project and allow the children the opportunity to evaluate themselves and each other, the interviews were videotaped on location.

Our media specialist made the interview appointments, transported the children during school hours to and from their prospective locations, and set up the portable videotape equipment. Prior to their interviewing and filming situations, our media man instructed the children about the equipment in terms of handling it, using it, and reacting to it. Each child who interviewed was accompanied by a team of two children who filmed the proceedings.

There are children who are not at all comfortable conducting an interview. Rather than chancing added frustrations for the shyer children, they were happily placed as cameramen. They became very adept at shooting porta-pak videotape cameras like miniature pros, at the same time witnessing the painless task undertaken by their interviewing peers.

Each interview lasted, on the average, seven minutes. Seven minutes may seem like a very short time when compared to professional interviews; however, seven minutes is an eternity for a child in this situation. It should be noted that the seven minute period was especially lengthy as the children did not have their questions written out completely. The children went out with a notecard carrying phrases or key words regarding the general topics that they had planned to cover through questioning. The children were compelled, then, to speak in a more or less impromptu manner, forming their questions as the interview progressed.

In a few cases their grammar faltered slightly, and in a few cases there was hesitation. But hesitation breeds thought, and mistakes lend themselves nicely to learning situations. Do we not learn by our mistakes? The children very obviously did. On several occasions, they came back thinking about what they might have said or done, an indication that they gained considerably from their experience.

When I initially discussed the idea with my superiors, I contended that there were many possibilities for the project in terms of related activities. As we went along, I found this to be true. At the onset, I suggested that the videotapes might be used for evaluation purposes in our classrooms and for career education at the elementary and junior high school levels. Indeed they may be. Further, rather than thanking those interviewed myself, I suggested that the children might send thank you notes to their subjects. At this point, we began a letter-writing unit to enable the children to communicate their appreciation by letter.

Interest on the part of the children, their parents, and the persons interviewed resulted in yet another activity. A tea was planned to give parents and interview subjects the opportunity to view the tapes. The children in our district have had many opportunities to view themselves on closed-circuit television, but many of their parents have never had such an opportunity. The tea provided the children with another opportunity to mingle with relatively unfamiliar adults, as well as to practice their letter-writing skills by writing letters of invitation. The tea was scheduled for American Education Week activities in the district, and was a resounding success.

EXIT DICK AND JANE?   Bonnie Dalzell

At first impression the fourth grade room in northeast Philadelphia's John Hancock School appears to be an ordinary classroom in the traditional elementary mold. Ubiquitous posters, hanging mobiles, and worktables laden with materials are typical and typically dominant. But then three less common features catch the eye. There is a television set which, while not unusual in today's classrooms, is being used in a most atypical way. The second feature is a list of terms used in television script writing—words like "pan," "cut to," "teaser," and "prop"—all neatly lettered on the blackboard. Feature three, a thick pile of mimeographed TV scripts resting on each student's desk, is really far out because the stapled pages are replacing the hallowed hardbound reader.

The fourth graders are in the middle of a reading lesson. Their teacher stands next to the TV monitor holding a script of "Brian's Song," a gripping story of two close friends, both professional football players, one of whom is dying. "Now that we've read the scene through," the teacher is saying, "I want you to think about the mood of the characters. Ask yourself how they really feel about themselves. How do they feel about each other? And pay close attention to the stage directions [instructions to the actors where and how to move] to see if the actors follow them to the letter."

The rustle of script pages is heard around the room as students flip back to the scene's opening. Then the teacher twists the TV knob, and the screen shows football player Gale Sayers walking into the hospital room of his friend Brian Piccolo. Except for occasional glances at the screen, the children keep their eyes fastened to the script. Later, when the bell rings for recess, they'll groan at the interruption. These concentrating youngsters are learning about making value judgments and strengthening whatever skills they already possess in this area. And they're enjoying it. What's more, the TV script technique helps other youngsters who have been reading below grade level make impressive gains which are reflected in improved reading achievement scores.

The script technique came out of the depths of one teacher's despair. From the first day Michael McAndrew walked into a classroom to teach a decade ago, he agonized over the reading problems of his academically weak students. These students had no physical or mental handicap to prevent their learning to read. Yet there they sat in his classroom, squirming restlessly in their chairs, stumbling over words on a page, nervously clearing their throats in the middle of a sentence, and looking invariably on the verge of stifling a yawn. Unreachable. Utterly impervious to blandishment, coaxing, and all the tricks in the bag of a natural teacher.

One day while he was mulling over another point—how important television had become to the American child—he had an idea. Why not use regular television programs as motivational tools to help poor readers? The children could use

Reprinted from *American Education* 12 (July 1976):9-13, courtesy of U.S. Department of Education and the author.

a script to read from while following the program on TV. The strategy sounded like heresy because it did away with that indispensable tool, the reading book. But Dr. McAndrew felt the idea might just be heretical enough to generate what, in his opinion, most poor readers lacked: motivation. Many of his students had been disenchanted early by the wooden characters of Dick and Jane and their obedient dog Spot. Instead of "seeing Spot run," they saw a page of dull words. These same students, he reasoned, loved Lucy, were galvanized by Ironside, and empathized with the characters in "Room 222." Why couldn't they read about them?

Convinced the idea deserved a try, Dr. McAndrew left the classroom in 1970 to join the staff of the Philadelphia school board. There he and a teaching colleague, Bernard Solomon, worked closely with then Deputy Superintendent Michael Marcase to draw up a proposal for using audiovisual equipment to reproduce TV programs on videotape. Once the programs were reproduced, scripts could be transcribed from the videotapes. The board approved the proposal and a program was born, with Dr. McAndrew as coordinator. Through the following months under the direction and supervision of Dr. Marcase, Dr. McAndrew and his staff painstakingly transcribed programs from sound to typed word, right down to the stage directions. Discussion exercises were also constructed for each scene of every script.

When the first script was finished, Dr. McAndrew carried copies of it into an urban classroom where three fourths of the students were reading below grade level. After going over the first scene in the script with the class, he wheeled in the television monitor and turned it on. As the students discovered the union of television with the printed word, they were at first stunned, then incredulous, and finally radiant. "They stared at the set, then down at the script, then back to the screen," recalls Dr. McAndrew. "Then all eyes went back to the script for the rest of the scene. They were turned on to reading."

The TV Reading Program began on a regular basis almost immediately in the Philadelphia schools. A serious problem right from the start has been one of containment. The program was designed originally for students in the middle grades 5-8 but soon expanded to reach those in grades 2-12 who have reading problems; however, it was not financially possible for every school in the district to have the program. Containment, though, hasn't been easy. "When one child says to another," Dr. McAndrew explains, "that he's reading 'Welcome Back, Kotter,' the child using a conventional reader is envious." Even in schools using the program (in its six years, over 50 Philadelphia schools have used the script technique), it has been necessary to restrict use to two or three classrooms over a six-month period.

At the outset many teachers were openly skeptical about substituting TV scripts for reading books, but when the technique worked for them they changed their minds. Exactly why it works is still somewhat of a mystery beyond the obvious appeal of TV. Even Dr. McAndrew is unable to explain why youngsters, given a choice of watching a TV screen or reading a script, invariably choose the latter. There were other surprises, too. Teachers who felt that students already behind in reading might find a technical vocabulary more than they could handle have found the opposite to be true; the special words, if carefully assigned, present few problems and capture interest. Also, habitual absentees began showing up in language arts classes when word about the scripts got around the school.

The word traveled swiftly to be picked up by the most unlikely receivers. One day Dr. McAndrew was approached in a school hall by a tough, street-wise teenager, the sort who would stalk out of a classroom if ever called upon to read anything aloud. "He was holding one of our scripts," Dr. McAndrew says, "and he blurted out, 'I can't read this but I want to.' He wasn't even in the TV Reading Program. I knew right then this was the bottom line of the program."

By the end of the first year, evidence about the program's effectiveness began coming in. For every year in TV Reading, a student gained at least a year and a half on his or her reading achievement score. A few older students who came into the program with very little motivation actually jumped three or four levels in a single year. But the key point was that no one in that first year gained less than a year and a half. Even in school systems outside Philadelphia that since have used the TV Reading Program — New York, Chicago, Jacksonville, and Los Angeles — test scores have matched the Philadelphia scores.

The achievement scores gave Dr. McAndrew a chance to face up to a confrontation he had been avoiding. A man of conscience, he had nonetheless been walking a tightrope. In transcribing the videotapes into scripts, he had not obtained permission from the writers, directors, and producers who held the various copyrights for the TV programs. All the reading program's success with poor readers could not excuse the fact that the transcriptions had been unauthorized. Now the problem had to be faced if the program were to continue.

With the full blessings of Dr. Marcase, Dr. McAndrew took a plane to Los Angeles to meet with the president of the National Academy of Television Arts and Sciences and with producers from the three networks. Balancing his confession of unauthorized use of TV programs with the solid news of improved reading scores, he begged permission to continue the program. He was hardly prepared for the reaction. Both the Academy officials and network producers were not only impressed enough to grant permission, but they went a step further, offering to supply any scripts he wanted.

Dr. McAndrew returned home bearing an exclusive agreement with the Academy and networks under which the Philadelphia School District would act as control center for other school systems wanting to adopt the technique and to use the growing library of videotapes and scripts. The agreement gave Dr. Marcase the green light for expanding the program beyond Philadelphia. To date, 3,500 school officials have made inquiries and paid visits. Appeal is particularly strong for schools in which Title I ESEA funding has supplied most of the equipment necessary to put the program into operation. Equipment needs are surprisingly modest: a videotape recorder, a TV monitor, and a few tapes which can be reused. Since a closed-circuit system is not required, the monitor can be a regular set with adapter. The total capital expenditure is approximately $1,100. Participating school systems can draw on Dr. McAndrew's library of 125 commercially made programs, 60 of which have accompanying scripts. It is even possible to get a program not in the library.

The basic lesson plan which Drs. Marcase and McAndrew have developed for using the TV scripts is clear-cut. The first session is spent skimming the script so that the characters and action can be introduced. Often a scene is "acted out." Selected vocabulary words are put on the board. Then the class views the program, although "viewing" here means following the script as the scene unfolds on the TV monitor. At various points the teacher freezes the picture to bring out a key idea, run over a difficult word, emphasize a facial expression, explain an idiom, or underline a crucial part of the action. Specific concepts are reviewed through mini-lessons, often accompanied by a special exercise to reinforce a skill that is being stressed. In the final phase any number of enrichment exercises can be devised to encourage the students to try some creative communication on their own. Students can write their own endings to a particular scene, they may draft ideas for "specials," or they may try to put together an original TV program.

The TV Reading Program has two firm rules. While students and teachers are invited to suggest programs, the final responsibility for selection rests with Dr. McAndrew. Programs with excessive violence or sex or with ethnic slurs are taboo. The ultimate test by Dr. McAndrew's standards is, "Would I want someone using this program to teach my own children?"

Ground rule two deals with the transcription process. In transcribing, the dialogue is never changed, but license is often taken with stage directions, putting them into full sentences to lend some language flexibility. "In rewriting directions," Dr. McAndrew explains, "we can create, for example, an enrichment lesson in alliteration."

Teachers working with the scripts have considerable flexibility in deciding how the tool will be used, and most work harder in exercising this latitude than they ever did in teaching with the conventional reading book. Few are prepared for the children's high level of motivation. Teacher Gerald Wernovsky, who team teaches in the TV Reading Program, admits, "Every once in a while I wish there were some easy teacher's guide to suggest various ways the TV reading program can be neatly folded into the total curriculum. But that's wishful thinking. I know the open-endedness of the program is its strongest point. Sure, I have to fight to keep at least two steps ahead of the children, and I'm being challenged to create exercises I'd never be able to attempt in a regular reading program. But I wouldn't have it otherwise."

If the program has a weakness, it is that the scripts and videotapes are raw materials, not finished products, and how they are handled is critical. The script technique can offer an exciting alternative for a good teacher to draw upon, but it cannot turn a poor teacher into a good one. Bea Univer, media assistant at Washington High, has watched many teachers use the technique. "Its effectiveness hinges on how good the teacher is," Mrs. Univer says. "If the teacher has prepared, then the excitement of the youngsters is something to see. If not, the experiment can turn into a mere babysitting stint."

Dr. McAndrew cautions teachers against another potential problem: the temptation to overteach a videotape. "You can 'kill' a script by making a session too pedagogic," he says, "so that the pace begins to drag. No more than 10 or 15 vocabulary words should be taken from a 30-page script, and it is best to introduce them three at a time as part of review sentences.

Many an educator has rested satisfied after maturing a fledgling idea into a full program. Not Dr. Marcase. Not Dr. McAndrew. With the script technique accepted into the Philadelphia schools, they began to improvise variations of it. They sought quality TV specials for the videotape and script library, realizing that though regular TV series fare like "Happy Days," "Gilligan's Island," and "Welcome Back, Kotter" would always form the bulk of the library, specials could form the substance. The first special they obtained was "The Autobiography of Miss Jane Pitman," followed by "Cyrano" in animated form, and then "Huck Finn," "The Cey," and Joseph Papp's production of "A Midsummer Night's Dream."

Once quality specials had become a regular part of the TV Reading Program, both men were ready for a new variation: having students read scripts in advance of a program's airing. They sought and got an ambitious first effort, the 400-page script for a three-hour documentary about the Cuban crisis, "Missiles in

October." The event also marked the first widespread interdisciplinary use of the TV Reading Program. Dr. McAndrew and his staff worked closely with George French, social studies director on the school board. The "Missiles in October" script was used in social studies classes involving 1,800 junior and senior high students throughout the Philadelphia School District. A 40-page workbook, prepared by William Brown, social studies chairman at Lincoln High, supplemented the script-reading.

The advance script made quite a stir in classrooms. "The students read the scripts as though they were copies of tomorrow's newspaper," says Dr. McAndrew. "There were heated classroom debates about Kennedy's decisions. Youngsters who normally sat mutely in class could not resist the fascination of decision-making at the highest levels." Although no actual assignment was made to watch the program, over 92 percent of the 1,800 students not only tuned in but stayed with it for the entire three hours.

Despite such drawing power, there remained that little nagging doubt. Was the TV script really a magnet that drew the students or was it just a splashy gimmick? Educators in one Philadelphia school developed a test for finding out. They began to make preparations for another television special. They psoted notices about the program throughout the school and took classroom time to urge students to watch it. Unlike the "Missiles in October" effort, however, they issued no scripts. A dismal 15 percent of the student body cared enough to watch the special. The message was clear; it was the script-reading in advance that made the difference.

Early this year the TV Reading Program took another unprecedented step by carrying the script idea beyond school walls. On the second Sunday and Monday nights of January, one of the networks presented James Costigan's television screenplay, "Eleanor and Franklin," based on the novel by Pulitzer Prize winner Joseph Lash. The program's sponsor gave the Philadelphia Board of Education enough funds to print a 16-page supplement of the entire script in the Philadelphia *Inquirer*. In the same issue, the newspaper carried a section giving enrichment exercises written by six English department members of the board.

The newspaper was then put into the hands of 125,000 secondary schoolchildren, with another 800,000 copies put on the doorsteps of Delaware Valley homes. It marked the first time that educational material of this kind had traveled to an audience outside of the schools.

Despite the carefully planned campaign, no one in the school district anticipated the community's response. Over 5,000 letters of congratulation and 1,800 equally enthusiastic phone calls swamped the school board office. The number of Philadelphia-area viewers impressed even the network: In the test area, "Eleanor and Franklin" had pulled a larger audience than the Superbowl game which had been aired at an earlier time.

In the letters and phone calls, parents reported that they were able to sit down at the dinner table and discuss something with their children that would be telecast in their living rooms that evening. Instead of the accustomed rush through dinner, families communicated. Fresh from classroom discussions, the children listened as their parents, full of memories about the FDR years, gave firsthand impressions.

The positive response opened up more possibilities. The network purchased the rest of Joseph Lash's books for the same high-quality adaptation that had been done with "Eleanor and Franklin." The sponsor who had underwritten the

Inquirer supplement now intends to expand to other city newspapers in the fall when more specials will be treated in advance.

Last but by no means least, the Philadelphia Board of Education, with a new-found power to guarantee audiences for quality programs, is beginning a role of influence in television programing. The role may well make education history. All three networks have been submitting scripts to Drs. Marcase and McAndrew, who will have input as to content in 25 percent of all specials aired this year.

And that covers a lot of ground for an idea that grew out of a teacher's despair and an administrator's sympathetic concern. The TV Reading Program is now reaching school districts all over the United States. The technique of having students read scripts in advance is established. Close cooperation is taking place between the Philadelphia School District and the networks over use of quality specials.

But neither Dr. Marcase nor Dr. McAndrew is one to rest on laurels. The fall season will bring another variation. The next public script-in-advance promotion, slated for this September, will involve newspapers and school districts in five major cities — Washington, New York, Chicago, Los Angeles, and San Francisco. There may even be a sixth, Boston. At the moment both educators are making their way through a pile of scripts to decide which script will be selected for the reading program.

For October, a second special will be highlighted, with five more cities added to the core group. A third is scheduled for November. By December when a fourth special will be promoted, at least 20 newspapers and school districts across the country are expected to participate in this unlikely union of television and the printed world.

For Dr. McAndrew, the teacher in program administrator's guise, the days are full and ideas keep coming. Those bleak memories of poor readers squirming captive in their chairs have faded from his mind. These days he sees young faces intently peering at television scripts; he wants other teachers to have the same experience.

I'M MY OWN TEACHER AIDE!   Dorothy Dutton

I don't imagine there is one teacher in one hundred who hasn't wished to be twins, to be able to be in two places at once. My listening center has made this wish come true for me. My own teacher-made tapes have made me my own teacher aide. And because I can be in two places at once, my listening post has become a valuable learning center, not just an entertainment area. While I am busy in one place teaching a reading group, for example, my tape is playing a preplanned lesson for another group.

Your recorder can do the same for you. The possibilities of teacher-made tapes are limited only by your imagination and the age and ability level of the children you may be working with.

Our first-grade children this year have listened to a variety of teacher-made tapes and really seem to be benefiting from the extra 15 to 20 minutes of instruction each day. The tape introducing new vocabulary for the next reading lesson is one of our favorites. The new words to be introduced are written at the top of a worksheet, allowing adequate space between words. Then on the tape, the words are introduced in the same manner as they would be in class. The children are instructed to mark vowel sounds, divide words into syllables, underline root words, circle endings, find initial consonant clusters, and put a box around the diagraphs. When the phonetic elements and the word meanings have been covered so that the children are familiar with the words, crayons are used to underline a certain word with a specific color or mark other words as requested. The bottom of the worksheet is used to encourage the children to use the words in sentences, use them to fill blanks, match words and definitions, or in some way use the new words meaningfully.

We have found this variety of tape to be helpful in a number of ways. The teacher can tell by looking at the pupil's markings on the worksheet how carefully he is listening and how well he comprehends and follows directions. A quick check in the reading circle will give the teacher a good indication of the student's retention of the new vocabulary. The tape can be stored on a three-inch reel to be reused when other students need that vocabulary. And a list of words any group finds difficult can be kept and a special tape prepared for additional practice.

Other areas of language development which can effectively be taped are drills on the formation of plurals, sentence construction, homonyms, opposites, and many more. In short, the tape recorder and headsets can help you become twins. They can become an extension of yourself.

Your tape recorder can also aid in the improvement of listening skills and comprehension. Tape a story, and then ask comprehension questions about it. The questions may be answered on a worksheet by circling the correct answer, by writing *yes* or *no*, or by completing a statement about the story. I have found that

Reprinted from *Instructor*, February 1974. Copyright © 1974 by The Instructor Publications, Inc. Used by permission.

children can be taught to evaluate their own listening skills with immediate self-correction.

Early primary children love to hear themselves read, and it is a valuable experience for them to listen to and evaluate their own oral reading. Tape a reading session, and then put the children on the headsets with their books. At the end of the tape, encourage them to read the story again, promising them they will have an opportunity to retape and listen once more. It is very rewarding to listen to and compare the two tapes which are made a day apart. Even the children are pleased and excited by how much they can improve in just one day.

One thing that is extremely difficult at the upper-grade level is scheduling with students individual discussions of themes or creative writing papers. Something approximating this may be accomplished on tape by dictating on a five-inch or seven-inch reel as you go over the student's paper. The listening can be done while you are working with other students. And it can be made continuous, the first student being directed at the end of his critique to turn off the recorder and ask the next student to come and listen to his section of the tape. A schedule listing the students and the numbers where their critiques begin is helpful in case a student wishes to listen a second time. Your having taken the time to discuss each paper will give the children a sense of receiving individual attention. Both the quality and the quantity of their writing will improve.

There are many people who look on the listening center as merely a gimmick, something to impress people with the school's modernity and the children's busyness. I find it a very valuable tool which can add hours to the teaching week.

II

MATHEMATICS AND SCIENCE

As elementary children develop the ability to communicate orally and begin to discover the relationship between alphabetical symbols arranged into words that eventually have meaning, they find that there is also a necessity to understand yet another language—mathematics. Most elementary teachers devote part of their instructional time daily for developing readiness and understanding in computation and problem solving. Complementing and reinforcing the concepts learned in the mathematics area is the world of science. The exploration of the "whys" asked by most children as they come into contact with the world around them is exciting and stimulating. Nonprint has been used in both areas by innovative teachers wishing to stimulate creative thought in their students.

Lola J. May in "Teaching Tools: How to Use Them in Math" goes beyond the tools most commonly considered in the teaching of math—the number line and Cuisenaire rods—to explain how she generates excitement with the overhead projector, tape recorder, 8mm film loop projector, and teaching machine. By using such hardware in her program she feels she has been able to bring action into the classroom. Mary Helen Youngs also reflects upon the advantages of using nonprint to generate excitement and participation in "8mm in the Science Program." Youngs explains how and why a sixth-grade teacher found the use of the 8mm projector beneficial in reinforcing a new "live science" curriculum.

Two of the authors in this section relate how they have utilized photography in the study of science. Robert H. Goldsmith sees the availability of simple-to-use instamatic cameras as an excellent way to tailor inquiry slides taken by the teacher or student for investigation and observation in the areas of geology, biology, ecology, and engineering. Julius F. Schillinger shows the steps he took to establish an entire curriculum for the Martha Holden Jennings Foundation in Cleveland, Ohio centered around the discovery of science through photography.

The final article in this section by Alan J. McCormack invites the adult educator to experiment with the willingness of youngsters to generate ideas, invent applications, and promote a tactile product he calls "wonderblob." Children in his activity-oriented proposal are encouraged to renew their creative imaginations and hold on to their ability to be idea machines for the future.

TEACHING TOOLS:
HOW TO USE THEM IN MATH

Lola J. May

It would be a mistake to say that teachers aren't using teaching tools in math. They are. What they're not doing for the most part is using these tools creatively.

I'm not talking about those teaching tools specifically designed for mathematics. There are, I'm happy to say, a growing number of teachers who are creating excitement in their math classes with such teaching aids as the number line and Cuisenaire rods. Fine. The more excitement we can generate in our math classes, the more mathematics our children will learn.

What I'm referring to are the familiar teaching tools like the overhead projector, the tape recorder and the teaching machine. They practically cry out for creative handling ... but when it comes to teaching mathematics, the cries all too often go unheard.

Take the overhead projector, for example. A teacher will sit down next to it and begin writing as she explains this or that mathematical operation. The children look at the screen and every so often the teacher looks up over her light at the children. The teacher's using the overhead projector to be sure, but as a substitute for the chalkboard, not as an avenue to creative teaching.

Certainly, the textbook will remain your primary teaching tool. But excitement is the name of the game, whether you're teaching mathematics or language arts or social studies. The sophisticated teaching tools available to us today can generate excitement, provided they're used creatively and not as a substitute for something else.

How can these tools be used creatively? Well, let's take a look at a few examples.

Overhead Projectors

First, there's the overhead projector. Its uses are many: Diagrams and models can be prepared ahead of time and shown at the opportune moment during the lesson. Multiplication facts can be graphically illustrated by drawing a 9 x 9 rectangular array and uncovering only those facts you want to demonstrate at a particular time; for example, 3 x 4 = 12 or 5 x 3 = 15 (see [Figure 1]). By making transparencies such as these, you'll be able to give the children daily multiplication drill with a minimum of effort.

In the primary grades, you can place on the projector three-dimensional objects such as jacks to be counted and placed in sets. While the activity is being projected at the front of the room, the children can follow the procedures with counters at their own desks.

[Figure 1]
Adapted from original.

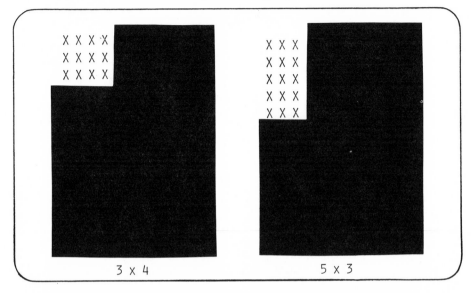

3 x 4   5 x 3

Here's another activity you can develop with the overhead projector: Draw two concentric circles with such numbers as 64, 144, 16, 40, 48 and 72 written in the inner circle (see [Figure 2]). Then, each day make up a different rule for your students to follow in filling in the outer circle. For example, if the rule were n + 4, the student would have to write in 68 in the appropriate section of the outer circle; if the rule were n ÷ 2, the correct answer would be 32.

[Figure 2]
Adapted from original.

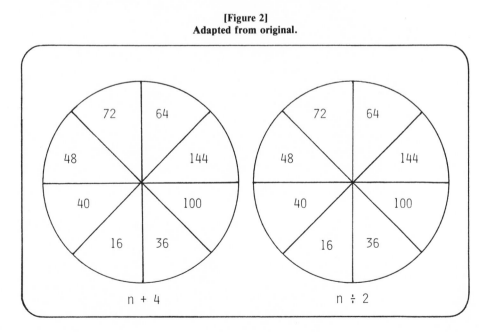

n + 4   n ÷ 2

There's one great advantage to using the overhead projector for reinforcement. Since you're facing the class, you're in a position for an on-the-spot evaluation of your youngsters' progress.

There are many transparencies produced commercially for mathematics study. But it's really just as easy to make your own. Just try a few and see what I mean.

Tapes and Film Loops

Tape recorders are an excellent means of reinforcement, especially when you're dealing with the auditory learner, the child who usually becomes bogged down with a lot of reading.

By programing the tapes—that is, by allowing intervals between the questions and answers—you can provide your youngsters with wonderful drill sessions on all of the basics of mathematics. It works this way: The student hears the question asked on tape and writes down his answer: then, after a suitable pause, the tape gives the correct answer, enabling the student to correct his answer. Since the student can do the drilling all by himself, there need never be the embarrassment of giving the wrong answer in front of the class.

As is the case with overhead projector transparencies, there are plenty of tapes available commercially—and plenty of opportunities to make your own.

For single-concept teaching, 8mm film loops can be used to maximum advantage. These colorful, animated loops provide mental pictures that are hard to forget. When film loops are used in a class presentation, the teacher can stop the action, ask questions and then continue when she's satisfied the children have grasped the point.

Film loops are even more effective when worksheets are prepared for use by the individual learner. You'll find that loops are especially good for students who have difficulty arriving at generalizations after seeing specific examples.

Teaching Machines

Complete programmed visual and audio presentations can be provided by a teaching machine. This machine will never replace *you*, of course—but it will make life a lot easier by enabling you to reach those students who just aren't "turned on" by chalkboard and textbook.

Many materials prepared for the teaching machine have built-in methods of diagnosing where a student needs to start and what kind of instruction and practice he needs to learn a skill or concept. The machine also provides tests to determine just what the student has learned.

Teaching machines accomplish a great deal more than just organized drill. They show ways of relating facts to other concepts and to families of facts. And since a correct response is immediately recognized, the machines provide instant reinforcement.

One good thing about a teaching machine is that the student is never intimidated. Even if he gives the wrong answer, the machine won't get angry or change its tone of voice. It will just repeat the same message over and over again until the right answer is given. How many teachers can claim the same measure of self-control?

Demonstration Materials

The more concrete the materials you bring into class, the more creative your teaching will be. For example, the "Count-A-Ladder," (EduKaid of Ridgewood) can be used to show sets of objects and number of sets. It's also useful in demonstrating the facts of addition, subtraction, multiplication and division.

An abacus can be used to teach place value. Youngsters can see, first hand, ten 1's being traded for one 10, or ten 10's being traded for one 100. And renaming in subtraction can be shown on the abacus where one 10 is changed to ten 1's, and so on.

The same materials used in class demonstrations can be used by some learners in doing their daily lessons. In so doing, they'll find these aids will help them develop a method of working out these problems.

What it all adds up to is that the role of the teacher is changing ... from instructor to guide. No longer can she stand in front of the class and just teach. Today she's expected to diagnose, prescribe and evaluate.

In order to handle these expanded functions, the teacher needs all the help she can get from the equipment and materials developed for education. Students will no longer be "turned off" by mathematics if the teacher can create action in the classroom. And making use of the materials and equipment at our disposal is surely the way to do it.

8mm IN THE SCIENCE PROGRAM

Mary Helen Youngs

Fairfax County School Board has embarked on an ambitious program of improving instruction. Innovation and experimentation are its theme.

As an example, a sixth-grade teacher at the Flint Hill Elementary School is creating a new curriculum which she calls "Live Science." It incorporates the disciplines of anthropology, sociology, economics, and physiology.

The first unit in anthropology is evolving into a successful program. Children are enthused by its exciting content. This class has been fortunate in having an 8mm projector and films to help reinforce learnings.

There are five advantages of an 8mm film projector. The machine is compact; it is easy to store; it is simple to operate; the films are inexpensive, making availability possible; and in using this medium the teacher is able to go in many directions and make her students a part of the action.

How do the children feel about using 8mm films? Let me quote:

"You can run the film over again without rewinding it. You can talk about it while it is showing pictures."

"You don't disturb other children when you watch this movie."

"I like this new projector because if you want to see it again it will run automatically. The clips are very interesting."

"We can see the archaeologist in real life and better understand what is going on."

In our Hollin Hall school, the 8mm projector has proved an effective device for developing the oral communication skills. When viewing in small groups with or without the teacher, the children discuss among themselves, arresting the frames or stopping the film temporarily to talk.

An 8mm film offers promising material for developing writing skills, both creative and functional, because it supplies one visual stimulus. The child, in the absence of verbal intake, has an opportunity to project in a unique way.

Mrs. Virginia Leighton, fourth-grade teacher, using an 8mm film loop "Lava Flows" (Film Associates, "Earth Science Series"), developed the study of factors affecting the structure of the earth — two types in live action photography — on the slopes of Mount Kilauea in Hawaii.

The class followed this by making a volcano. The film loop was motivational and served as research material for committee reporting.

The teacher notes that it invited further investigation by raising many questions in children's minds, to which many sought answers in visits to the media center.

In small-group viewing, the teacher learned much about students from their comments. In this instance, insight was gained not only into the quality of communication but also into the cognitive level at which the child was operating and the diversity among children in the quality of their understanding of cause-and-effect relationships.

PERSONAL INQUIRY SLIDES   Robert H. Goldsmith

The use of slides in the classroom is not uncommon. It may be difficult to find commercial inquiry slides that integrate easily into a lesson plan and which are relevant to the teacher's or student's immediate experience. Now, however, with the relatively inexpensive and simple-to-use instamatic cameras, it becomes easy for anyone to line up his desired picture or slide, press the button, and have his negative developed.

Besides the ease of taking slides, there are decided classroom benefits. The teacher has the opportunity to raise questions for an investigation or to work with students in the art of observation. There is a sense of drama obtained with a slide that cannot be obtained using the same scene in a book. Enthusiasm can easily result from the teacher's enjoyment of sharing an experience. Interest is enhanced especially if local sites can be found which offer inquiry situations. Disadvantages include the problem of timing to hold interest and the need to set the stage by providing background or needed information.

Use of personal inquiry slides gives one a wide choice of situations but some are especially desirable. The scene should raise the teacher's curiosity or interest or give a dramatic illustration of an event in which the teacher thinks his students might be interested.

Geological, biological, environmental, and engineering items are best suited for this inquiry approach. After choosing an appropriately interesting inquiry scene, center your camera on the main point of emphasis. Competition from other items should be avoided. Having a person in the scene might add appeal but the viewer's attention may center there rather than upon the desired point. Choose the time of day carefully since the light intensity and some physical phenomena will both be influenced by your choice. Personal inquiry slides an be used by the teacher in many different approaches and programs, from traditional to individually paced.

Reprinted by permission of *Science and Children* 9 (April 1972):20. Copyright © 1972, *Science and Children* magazine.

SCIENCE THROUGH PHOTOGRAPHY   **Julius F. Schillinger**

A high percentage of what children learn is learned through the eye. They see television and other man-made visuals so much that they vastly prefer to get their entertainment and learning through these media. Consequently, it is now more difficult to provide adequate learning opportunities solely by word of mouth (or print).

Recognizing these factors, and realizing that their efforts to reach today's visual child with traditional nonvisual methods is increasingly ineffective, many schools and other groups concerned with education have embarked upon visual literacy programs. Students in these programs spend considerable time in planning, taking, arranging, and using self-made photographs and sequences of photographs for the intentional communication of meaning.

Until recently, such programs have primarily been built into the reading and language arts curricula only. But children have a bank of environmental experiences which are probably never adequately tapped by many science curricula. Why not encourage the child to go to that portion of his visual experience that he knows best, his community, his world—to involve him in science concept building experiences also? Why not place in his hands a device that allows him to conceptualize his ideas and share the excitement of discovery? And why not then use what he has recorded as the basis for his own personal set of learning materials?

In an attempt to respond to these needs, the Martha Holden Jennings Foundation of Cleveland, Ohio awarded the author an educational grant for the development of a science-oriented photography program during the summer of 1972. After the purchase of darkroom supplies and an Instamatic camera for each of the 16 sixth-graders in the program, the following activities were incorporated into the project:

1. Students learned the entire photographic process from the use of the camera to the development of the negative and final print; this began with an introduction to the simple pinhole camera.

2. Students were supposed to use the camera as a "third eye" to record visually a particular portion of a whole thing they saw. When their pictures were printed, they were encouraged to verbalize about what they had recorded.

3. Three areas of elementary science were stressed: light energy, conservation of natural resources, and the animal kingdom.

Reprinted by permission of *Science and Children* 11 (September 1973):33-35. Copyright © 1973 *Science and Children* magazine.

4. Field trips were taken to allow the child to explore, visually record, read, and talk about the world beyond his immediate neighborhood and classroom.

5. Students composed slide presentations which utilized the work of the entire group to build a story about various scientific concepts by combining slides and experiences. One result was a group composition for presentation to other science classes.

6. Visual-verbal science textbooks were created by each child by writing their stories visually with still black and white photographs they had taken with their cameras and then mounted. Oral descriptions accompanying each picture were recorded on tape and later written into the child's book.

In the preliminary study of the use of the camera, students found that the amount of light an object reflects is dependent upon its color and its proximity to the light source. For example, when taking pictures of dark colored objects, they either had to increase the amount of light or move closer to the subject for best results. Through the use of the pinhole camera, the students learned that the image of their subject would be recorded in an upside-down manner. They correctly concluded that light must travel in straight lines. To reinforce this concept, the children were taught to use the technique of "bounce flash." When the flash was aimed at an angle up to the ceiling, students observed that the top of the subject would be illuminated if it was at a corresponding angle to the direction of the flash.

During the second week of the program, the class toured Cleveland's industrial "Flats" area, the site of some of the major industries in northeastern Ohio. By means of the camera, they recorded events which they deemed significant to environmental awareness. Pictures of air and water pollution in the area resulted. After being mounted, they served as a focus for discussion and constant reminder of existing environmental problems. The shores of Lake Erie provided an opportunity to view the results of these problems. Students were amazed at the quantity of dead aquatic life along various regions of the shoreline. Three different species of fish were observed and photographed as they were washed up on the shores of the lake. Two students took one of the dead fish back to the classroom for dissection and further study.

Some positive aspects of the environment were also photographed on field trips to state parks in Ohio and in the Adirondack Mountains of New York State. A student, seeing a wild deer for the first time in his life, suggested that a photographic study of animals be attempted. Finding it difficult to photograph many animals in their natural habitat, the class decided that a trip to the Cleveland Zoo would give them a chance for close-up pictures of animals they had not yet observed. Many pictures were taken and after being mounted on cardboard they were classified by the children according to the various characteristics observed in the pictures. Several of the pictures were enlarged and are presently being used in our school's science program.

The fact that Charles W. Chesnutt School has incorporated photography into the science program and plans to expand its use attests to the program's success with youngsters. Teachers and schools wishing to undertake a similar program need not have an extensive background in photography. For example, although a completely equipped darkroom was an integral part of Chesnutt School's five-week summer project, it can be replaced by inexpensive processing envelopes in which students put their exposed film to be developed by a local photofinisher. The camera itself is a miniature darkroom which can be the source of many exciting scientific experiments by the children. Why are lenses important to the camera? Does it make any difference as to how long the shutter remains open? Is the aperture (opening) in all cameras the same? Why not? How does the aperture in adjustable cameras compare to the pupil of our eye? These are just a few of the ideas that students may be curious about. There are many more.

Summary

Photographs are a major part of our day-to-day experience. We are surrounded by photographs of the world around us — still, or on movies and TV. "So, nothing could be more exciting or real for children," as John Holt has said, "or rich in ways of moving out into the world, than learning how to use and using cameras." Give a child a camera and some film. Turn him loose in his own world. Let him draw upon his own experience to record nature — the world — as he sees it and watch what happens.

References

1. Eastman Kodak Company. *Elements of Visual Literacy*. Kodak Publication t-25. 1969.

2. Holt, John. "Photography and Writing." *What Do I Do Monday?* E. P. Dutton and Company, Inc., New York City. 1970. p. 201.

Sources of Additional Information on Photography Programs

1. Center for Visual Literacy, College of Education, The University of Rochester, New York 14623.

2. Coordinator, Education Projects, Department 624, Eastman Kodak Company, Rochester, New York 14650.

3. Schillinger, Julius F., John F. Kennedy Schule, 1 Berlin 37 (Zehlendorf) Teltower Damm 87-93, West Berlin, Germany.

WONDERBLOB AND THE
IDEA MACHINES

Alan J. McCormack

We are, all of us, born as "idea machines." We have a built-in program inside urging us to both produce and consume ideas—that's what makes us human. The very young have a strong sense of humor and a rich fantasy life. Children at play are ultimate idea machines. Youngsters create a world of their own or rearrange the existing world in a way that is pleasing. And don't think for a minute that children do not take the world seriously. Play is serious work for young idea machines.

Unfortunately, idea machines do not necessarily improve with age. They tend to rust, and their once smooth-running gears jam with crusty too-formal logic and "I can't do it" attitudes. Instead of generating and voraciously consuming new ideas, mature idea machines worry about "What's wrong with this idea?" This is all very sad, because now, more than ever, we need fully functioning idea machines to solve problems of pollution, famine, loneliness, war, energy, and greed.

What's to be done? Idea machines become sluggish and rusty because they are not treated as idea machines. They are treated more like copying machines, learning how to accurately reproduce all materials fed into them. We need to treat youngsters more like the idea machines they are, and not promote the almost inevitable sluggishness. How? By providing school experiences aimed at, charged by, and overflowing with opportunities for idea production. Occasionally, a lesson should become an Idea Circus with idea machines creating, combining, and multiplying *ideas.*

One of the problems we adults have is that the familiar becomes just too familiar. Reexperience, with your class, what it is like to encounter a material for the first time—like the first time you ate Jello or smelled newly cut grass. At this stage of experience with an object, it *is* strange, and you'll be amazed at how this causes idea machines to automatically mesh, switch on, focus, and invent.

What material could do this? I call it "Wonderblob." Wonderblob is made from a new plasticlike, water-soluble polymer. Its trade name is "Polyox Water-Soluble Resin." Used widely as an additive to manufactured products, but little known in its pure state, Wonderblob sparkles with curious properties. Wonderblob is concocted by simply mixing Polynox concentrate (a fluffy white powder) in warm water.

Wonderblob looks like a hybrid brew of raw egg whites, hair setting lotion, and rubber cement. Having a water base, you can easily dye it any hue with food colors. One of its more attractive qualities as a subject of scientific study for youngsters is that it is entirely nontoxic and nonallergenic. It's a good policy to insist that kids *never* taste unknown substances, but you don't have to worry if someone accidentally (or in a burst of overcuriosity) happens to eat some.

Wonderblob is peculiar stuff. When you start pouring it from one container to another, it just won't stop. Put your finger in it — when you take it out, you'll find a long sticky string will follow. Try mixing it with household substances (salt, sugar, and so on), and you'll find it to be an excellent solvent. And it has almost mysterious friction-reducing properties. If a very small amount of Wonderblob (less than 1%) is added to water, the water can be pumped through a hose with friction reduced by 40% to 60%! Used this way it is known as UCAR Rapid Water Additive and helps firemen deliver water faster.

In thicker concentrations, Wonderblob is used in industrial preparation of adhesives, paints, cosmetics, toothpaste, and soap. A high-flying variety is used in stabilizing deicing fluids of aircraft!

But, let's get back to our Idea Circus. An unfamiliar substance like Wonderblob (or some other newly developed substance) can be used as a trigger to turn on the idea machines in your classroom. One way to begin is with a class fantasy trip. Set the stage for it by dimming the classroom lights and having everyone sit back and relax, or even lie on the floor. Slowly, with a soothing voice, stimulate the imagination with these words.

Close your eyes and be comfortable ... pretend that your mind is getting very clear ... you can think better than you ever could before ... now you see yourself walking down a path to a cave ... inside the cave is a very wise person who motions for you to enter ... he has two gifts for you ... the first is a strange liquid he has in a large bottle ... "This is a Wonder Liquid," he says.... "you must find out all you can about its properties ... touch the liquid ... how does it feel?" ... The Wise Person gives you a second gift ... you don't see anything, but you feel different ... your brain begins to tingle ... "I have given you great brainpower," says the Wise Person, ... "you are now an idea machine ... use your new power to learn about the liquid I have given you."

Then, unveil some Wonderblob. Explain (tongue-well-in-cheek, of course!) that this is the Wise Person's Wonder Liquid. So, the Idea Circus begins!

Ring One — Generating Ideas

Provide the kids with small dollops of Wonderblob on plastic food wrap. Give them some time to learn about Wonderblob's properties. You can expect the usual chorus of "Yech!" "Gross!" and "Ne-e-eat!"

After initial curiosities are satisfied, remind the youngsters that they are idea machines and obliged to find out all they can about the fluid. Teach them the standard brainstormer's trick of withholding evaluation of ideas until a lot of ideas are gathered; they'll be more likely to come up with unusual ideas. Divide the class into investigation groups, have them dream up as many questions as they can for scientific study of Wonderblob, then help them select a few of their ideas and launch some experiments. Here are some questions for probing the nature of Wonderblob.

What can our senses tell us about Wonderblob's properties? (How does it look, feel, smell, sound — but not taste!)

What will float in Wonderblob?

Does Alka-Seltzer dissolve in Wonderblob? If so, how does the dissolving time compare with that of water?

What else will dissolve in Wonderblob? Water? Oil? Salt? Flour?

How heavy is it? How does its weight compare with other liquids?

Does it evaporate? If so, is anything left behind?

How "stringy" is Wonderblob? (Measure the length of "strings" left behind a finger touched to the liquid and then moved upward.)

How "runny" is Wonderblob? (Make a cardboard incline covered with aluminum foil. Have a contest among drops of Wonderblob and other liquids running down this surface.)

How "sticky" is Wonderblob? (Compare the pull it requires to remove a small flat square of plastic from Wonderblob's surface with the pull required to remove the same object from other liquid surfaces.)

How does Wonderblob's rate of absorption into a paper towel compare with other liquids?

Ring Two—Inventing Applications

Now that kids understand some of the qualities of the material, see what uses they can think up.

One youngster proposed shallow troughs of Wonderblob on factory assembly lines. Another engineered a Better Thief Trap to protect her home. Frozen as a disc, Wonderblob has been recommended as an ideal low-friction hockey puck. For maintaining law and order without guns and tear gas, how about spraying rioters with a Wonderblob solution? They would slip, slide, and swear—but they certainly wouldn't be able to carry on a proper riot!

An easy-to-brush, nondrip paint is an attractive product for the do-it-yourself handyman. Wonderblob-coated "easy swallow" pills might be a boom to youngsters with reluctant throats. You can always convert your water bed to a Wonderblob bed!

Many kids will have a good time coming up with ideas such as these. A few will even try them out. The important thing is that creative juices are flowing and the Idea Circus is in full swing.

Ring Three—Madison Avenue!

The professional "Ad Men" have inflicted the Pet Rock, Screaming Yellow Zonkers, and "Plop-plop, Fizz-fizz" on American society. Here is a chance for your class to strike back while completing a legitimate language arts project. Kids can develop advertisement posters to "sell" some of the more unusual applications they dream up for Wonderblob.

Lest you think I have gone "bonkers" myself, I should point out that humor is considered a creative process by psychologists. Episodes of humor are mentally developed by processes very much like those involved in insight or invention. And, a high correlation has been found *not* between creativity and intelligence, but between creativity and sense of humor. So, a humor-ladened activity *is* appropriate for the third ring of an Idea Circus.

Although I've conveyed a whimsical approach to children's creative development, I believe this should be one of our greatest concerns. I secretly weep when young adults tell me they "just can't come up with ideas" and "can't see any value" in fantasy. Many of our school experiences grind down, discourage, laugh at, or otherwise thwart the natural creative tendencies of idea machines. By the end of a college education, many are no longer idea machines — just this-is-the-*right*-way-you-should-do-it machines.

Albert Einstein would be unhappy. He once remarked: "Imagination is more important than knowledge."

III

ART AND MUSIC

The use of art and music in the elementary curriculum have long been recognized by educators as a means for a child of this age to express creativity visually and orally. Both appear to serve the purpose of promoting the total growth of the child by providing an opportunity for creative expression.

Betty J. Swyers attests to the success her class had with an art project using coin holders and translucent paints to make a slide show as a background for dancers to perform with recorded music, all conceptualized by her students. She goes on to give a number of helpful hints on how to make other art slide variations using inexpensive materials. Anne D. Modugno, in "Electronic Creativity in the Elementary Classroom" compares the discovery process the children experienced in making their own music with that of artist filling a canvas: "Like an artist with a blank canvas, [children] should have a blank tape and use their creative potential to fill it." Modugno shows how elementary children can make their own original electronic music by using a simple tape recorder to manipulate preselected sounds. Although not mentioned in this article, the reader who wishes to experiment with electronic creativity might wish to rent a copy of Weston Woods' movie "Where the Wild Things Are" and "The Picture Book Animated" to hear and see how the sound track was manipulated to achieve the desired affects.

SLIDE INTO ART

Betty J. Swyers

At the end of each week, a teacher I know hands her students a cassette tape recorder and sends them off to a nice quiet corner to record their reactions to the classroom program. During the weekend, as she goes about the weekend chores, the teacher carries the tape recorder from place to place and listens to the playback. The following transcript is representative of the kind of message she receives:

"Hi! This is your old friend Roger back again and I guess you're dying to know how we made those gorgeous slides you saw today when you came back after we had art with Mr. Shull [the school's art specialist].

"Mr. Shull told us last week that we'd do something really fantastic today. But when he came in the door, instead of being loaded down with all that stuff he is usually lugging around, all he had was one little brown paper sack. He put the sack on the table and made a big production out of taking the stuff out of the bag one thing at a time. There were five bottles of ink which were, ah, green, yellow, red, white and, ah, oh yeah, blue. There were two more bottles of another different kind of ink which turned out to be crystal paint like you paint on the back of fish tanks — really neat stuff. Then he took out a bunch of coin holders, which we knew were coin holders because lots of us are coin collectors, a roll of clear plastic and some cotton swabs.

" 'Does anybody have any idea what we're going to make with this stuff?' he asked.

"Everybody always has lots of ideas and some of them were really dumb but nobody guessed.

" 'Well, in about 15 minutes,' he says, 'we're going to put on a spectacular slide show and you're going to produce the slides.'

" 'Fifteen minutes,' we said. 'It took you longer than that to pass the stuff out.'

"But we made slides all right, and you saw how fantastic they turned out. They were so simple even a baby could make them.

"All we did was stick the tip of our finger in the bubbles at the top of the ink and then fingerpainted on the plastic. Or else we swabbed some of that crystal paint on — that gave those slides a neat, frosty look. Then we blew on them to make them dry faster. We put them in the coin holders, rubber cemented the holders closed, and there was our slide ... except we had to trim one edge to make it fit easy in the projector tray.

"Now I got this really great suggestion for next week. We can bring our records and record some of the best music and put the projector way in the back of the room so the picture will be real big on the wall, and then we can let the girls

Reprinted from *Grade Teacher* 89 (October 1971):30-31, 34. Copyright © 1971 by Macmillan Professional Magazines. Used by permission of The Instructor Publications, Inc.

be go-go dancers in front of the picture and we can invite the principal down for the show."

Slide-making is indeed a "neat" experience that guarantees fantastic results and unexpected responses (especially after the principal arrives for the go-go show) and it is simple to do. The materials are inexpensive. Coin holders (the silver dollar opening size) cost somewhere in the vicinity of 49¢ for a package of 25, and are cheaper when purchased in hundred lots. They are worth the investment for the first attempts. Later the students can cut their own frames from lightweight cardboard such as shirt boards.

The ink is a special transparency ink which is not only translucent but will adhere to the acetate. It comes in a wide choice of colors and sells at art supply stores for around 55¢ a bottle.

Crystal paint can be purchased in pet shops or in dime and department stores which stock aquarium supplies. It comes in a variety of colors, and sells for approximately 59¢ a jar.

Here are some project variations:

For special effects, deliberately seal the frame and project the slide while the inks are still wet. The movement on the screen is fascinating and leads into some imaginative story telling.

"Perpetual motion" can be obtained by sealing a drop of oil in the frame on top of well-dried inks. The heat from the projector lamp will cause it to keep moving.

For silhouettes, seal various small objects between two layers of acetate. These can be cut-out images, or "found" objects.

For an ethereal "Jack Frost" effect, swab crystal paints only on the acetate. Dry thoroughly before sealing because it is only after the crystal paint dries that the patterns appear.

Paint crystal paint on one side of the acetate, inks on the other.

Paint crystal paint on both sides of the acetate. Then, while the paint is still sticky, add drops of food coloring.

Paint one side of acetate with India ink, the other with transparency inks or crystal paint. Scratch away part of the inks to produce colorful "fireworks" effects.

Apply inks with toothpicks to form lines.

Instead of clear acetate, try the colored kind found in theme folders. Swab with crystal paint. Dry thoroughly for intricate frosty patterns.

Drop tiny bits of colored art tissue on acetate, sprinkle with water and watch dyes escape.

Use felt pens to make designs, images and words such as "The End."

Put string designs on wet inks before sealing frames.

ELECTRONIC CREATIVITY
IN THE ELEMENTARY CLASSROOM

Anne D. Modugno

Are music programs in the elementary schools offering students exciting and challenging creative experiences? Children at this level *can* be motivated to create and develop in their own way. Like an artist with a blank canvas, they should have a blank tape and use their creative potential to fill it.

In an art class, the child develops a personal understanding of shape, line, color, and texture as he begins to create. He must decide which colors to use and how to change colors without losing certain effects. He experiences the fun of finding another world and then finding himself in the middle of it.

Elementary school children can also find another world in music by enjoying the experience of transforming raw materials into finished musical compositions. They should be given the chance to use a wide variety of sound materials, manipulating and structuring them so they assume new meanings. In doing so, children develop an understanding of shape (musical form), line and color (timbre), and texture. They decide what sounds to use, how to change sounds, and how to relate sounds so they become meaningful.

Electronic music, with its multitude of modifications and diverse sounds, is a contemporary idiom that can foster such creative activity. The individual is not intimidated by the traditional problems of having to read and understand musical notation. Electronic music has no quarter notes, G clefs, and key signatures. Yet it is an art that demands imagination, develops the desire and ability to explore and investigate new ideas, and challenges the student to use newfound knowledge in a new venture. The pupil learns to think, to wonder, to be wrong, to be right. Flexibility and freedom are basic concepts; nobody dictates but the creator himself.

At the elementary school level, pupils are able to use the tape recorder in a creative way. By means of two stereo tape recorders, pupils can record a limitless number of natural or "concrete" sounds. Once they have explored all the tape recorder's capabilities, they can manipulate and modify recorded sounds into meaningful musical sequences. Teachers should encourage them to experiment with the sounds they find appealing and interesting and guide them in shaping these sounds into a conceptually acceptable composition.

The ingredients for a good melodic and/or rhythmic line are the same for the tape recorder as for wind, string, or percussion instruments. An interesting line has tensions, releases, repetitions, contrasts, and sequences. Sounds must be shaped by the composer just as a sculptor shapes clay. The tape recorder becomes the composer's tool. With it he can get many shapes in pitch, loudness, and tone color.

Practical tape work is the core of the electronic music program. The pupil needs to record a variety of sounds: vocal, instrumental, oral (such as snapping

Reprinted by permission of the author and *Today's Education* 60 (March 1971):62-64.

the tongue against the palate), and percussive (such as striking different materials or tapping the microphone). Once the sounds are recorded, pupils can manipulate them with no more equipment than two tape recorders.

Speed change effects many variations of recorded sounds. If a sound is recorded at 7½ ips (inches per second) and played back at 3¾ ips, the tape will move at half the speed, and sounds will be an octave lower. Pitch, duration, and timbre change when the original sound is played at a different speed. With the use of two tape recorders, the original sound may be recorded to sound several octaves higher or lower. Let the pupils try out the following:

• Play the original sound at a slower speed than that used for recording it. Record the slower sound on a second tape recorder — at a faster speed. Play this copy at the slower speed and once again record at the faster speed. This process will lower the original sound several octaves. If the procedure is reversed, the sounds will be heard several octaves higher.

• Experiment with dynamic levels through volume control. Manipulate the volume controls to produce changes in dynamic levels. Record on one recorder while changing levels on another and listen to the playback.

• Move the reels manually while they are on the tape recorder. Put the control knob in forward position and take the tape away from the capstan. Manipulate the tape by hand and listen to the new sounds as the tape moves at different speeds (see Figure 1 [page 53]).

• Play a recorded tape backwards. This can be done by recording on a stereo and playing back on a monaural recorder.

An important part of electronic music is the use of tape loops. A tape loop may be made from a short section of recorder tape by splicing the end to the beginning. The sound on the loop is repeated over and over.

On a stereo tape recorder, record a sound on channel I and another sound on channel II. Then record both these sounds onto a single channel of another recorder. This leaves opportunity to add more material on the other channel.

By avoiding the erase head, it's possible to create sound on sound on one channel. Several layers of sound may be recorded this way. Figure 2 [page 53]shows one way to avoid the erase head.

Splicing and editing have extensive potential. Attacks made by percussion instruments may be cut out. Sequences of sound may be interchanged. Part of a musical sequence may be spliced out.

All these techniques can be further modified in conjunction with electronic music equipment. The most common electronic instruments can be used — the electronic organ and the electric guitar, piano, and Autoharp. By means of a simple adapter, all of these can be plugged directly into most tape recorders.

An inexpensive electronic music lab is now on the market. It has a complete basic set of eight electronic instruments that are small enough for children to hold in their hands. The instruments may be played individually, in groups, or all at once.

Listening to numerous recordings helps introduce the young student to electronic music sounds. The following recordings offer a variety of source sounds:

"Dripsody" by LeCaine. Folkways. FM3436/FMS33436.

"Bowery Bum" by Mimaroglu. Turnabout. TV 34004S.

"Piece for Tape Recorder" by Ussachevsky. CRI. 112.

"Evolutions—Ballet Suite" by Badings. Epic. BC 1118.

"Switched-On Bach" by Carlos. Columbia. MS 7194.

"Gesang der Jünglinge" ("Song of the Children") by Stockhausen. Deutsche Grammophon. 138811.

Electronic music encourages students to be creative and involves them in "thinking sound." Pupils are challenged as they face the task that all composers must deal with—that of manipulating sound in a meaningful way. For starters, they can conduct the experiment described below, all of which can be done with one or two tape recorders.

Note: In the diagrams (Figures 1-5) that follow, only those parts of the tape recorder that are relevant to the discussion are shown. Also, all the experiments—except the one illustrated in Figure 3—can be performed on older model tape recorders that have two heads (one for erasing and one for both recording and playing back). A more recent model, with separate heads for recording and playing back, must be used for the Figure 3 experiment.

• Fast record, slow playback. (a) Set recorder speed at 7½ ips. (b) Gently wind several feet of tape onto take-up reel. (c) Set tape counter at 000. (d) Plug in microphone and record series of sounds. (e) Rewind tape to 000. (f) Play back tape at 7½ ips. (g) Rewind tape to 000 and play back at 3¾ ips. Ask: What differences do you hear?

• Slow record, fast playback. (a) Set recorder speed at 3¾ ips and repeat steps b, c, d, and e as listed on page 63. (b) Play back tape at 3¾ ips. (c) Rewind tape to 000 and play back at 7½ ips. Ask: What differences do you hear?

• Recording fast rewind and fast forward playback. (See Figure 3.) (a) Set recorder at 7½ ips. (b) Gently wind several feet of tape onto take-up reel. (c) Set tape counter at 000. (d) Plug in microphone and record low notes on piano, guitar, or Autoharp at extremely slow speed for two minutes. Do *not* rewind. (e) Place tape behind tape lifter. (Tape lifters, which are used in comparatively inexpensive machines, eliminate signal playback during fast forward or fast rewind.) (f) Rewind and listen to changes while tape rewinds. (g) Play fast forward with tape still behind tape lifter. (When recording be sure signal [sound] is recording at very high level.)

• Octave change, using two tape recorders. (This process not only changes the pitches but doubles the length of the recorded sound in each step.) (a) Set recorder at 7½ ips. (b) Gently wind several feet of tape onto take-up reel. (c) Set tape counter at 000. (d) Plug in microphone and record series of percussive sounds. (e) Rewind tape to 000. (f) Play back at 3¾ ips. (g) Record percussive sounds on second recorder at 7½ ips while playing recorder #1 at 3¾ ips. (h) Play copy on recorder #2 at 3¾ ips and record on #1 at 7½ ips. (i) Continue process at least two more times; listen to final result. (If procedure is reversed, sounds will be heard several octaves higher.)

• Hand manipulation of reels. (See Figure 1.) (a) Thread recorded tape on recorder. (b) Take tape away from capstan. (c) Put control knob in forward position. (d) Manipulate reels by hand.

• Hand manipulation of reels. (See Figure 4.) (a) Thread tape in front of playback head alone. (b) Hand-manipulate tape, pulling it sideways across head. (c) Listen to signal as it is pulled slowly and ask: What pitch variables are there?

[Figures 1–5]

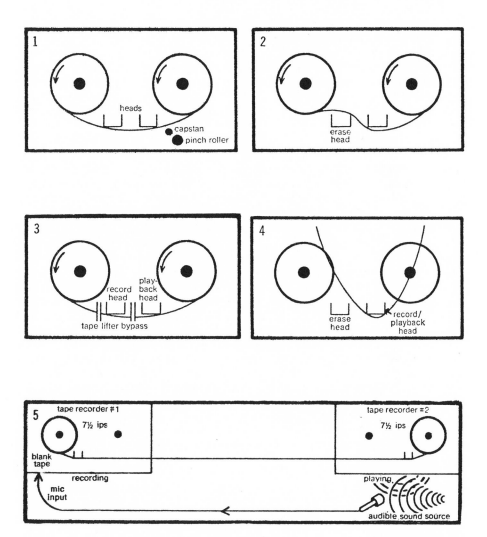

• Experiment with tape loop, using these materials: splicing bar, splicing tape, recording tape, razor blade, wax crayon.

(a) Locate desired sound on tape and mark beginning and end of sound with wax crayon. (b) Gently pull marked section of tape forward and place it on splicing bar. (c) Using wax crayon, mark with an arrow the direction of the sound. (d) Place mark which indicates beginning of sound on diagonal line of splicing bar. (e) Cut tape on diagonal with razor blade. (f) Do the same with the mark which indicates end of sound. (If abrupt sound is desired, use vertical splice.) (g) With shiny side facing up, carefully place ends of tape together, making sure there is no gap. (h) Cut a piece of splicing tape about ¾ of an inch in length. (i) Place splicing tape across ends of recording tape. (j) Gently remove loop from splicing bar. (k) Place loop on tape recorder and listen to repeated sound. (A successful tape loop will not have audible click at point of splice.) (l) Experiment with speed change. (m) Place loop, with dull side out, on tape recorder. (The sound is being played backwards.) (n) Put a band of paper with description of sound and direction on the loop.

• Experiment with simple echo reverberation (delayed feedback), using two tape recorders. (See Figure 5.) (a) Place blank tape on one tape recorder. (b) Gently wind several feet of tape onto take-up reel. (c) Place take-up reel on second recorder with tape passing in front of heads on both recorders. (d) Set tape counter at 000. (e) Set same speed on both recorders. (f) Plug microphone into first recorder with record buttons down. (g) Recorder #2 should be in play position. (h) If recorders are not synchronized (tape lags), move tape away from capstan on recorder #1. Note: The volume controls of both machines, plus the distance the microphone is held from the speaker of #2, all determine the volume and quality of the echo. A large tape loop may be used if you do not care to save the finished product. The distance between the recorders determines the time lapse of the echo.

IV

PRODUCTION OF MATERIALS IN THE
MEDIA CENTER AND CLASSROOM

The production of materials by students has been recognized by more and more teachers and media specialists as providing a valuable learning experience. During the planning and production process, students are called upon to select suitable topics and the medium most appropriate for visual display, to interact with peers, to visualize in a logical sequence what will eventually be projected, to operate all types of equipment, and perhaps most important, to become *active* participants in their own learning. Materials produced may be used in many cases for instruction in the classroom or for reference in the media center.

The first article in this section by Elise Wendel speaks to the reluctance of some media specialists to try local production, but shows how valuable such an experience can be for students in developing organizational skills and in motivating them to read over the chosen subject. Wendel's group of students were fourth to sixth graders. Robert T. Gasche in "Yes, They Can Make Slides, Use a Dry Mount Press, and More" reflects on producing materials with an even younger group—kindergarteners. Throughout his article, he recounts the enthusiasm the children expressed and the understanding they had of the process. Andd Ward Cipriano agrees in her article that young students are capable of selecting magazine pictures, sequencing them, and taping a story about the pictures. Her activity was designed to foster creativity and provide a storytelling experience with second graders.

In Hetty Cramer's article, she explains how her fourth grade class made their own original fantasy on film, and the benefits she and the entire group reaped in the process. Whereas Cramer's discussion is limited to making live-action super 8mm movies, Ed Price in "Filmmaking in the Classroom: Scratching on Film" adds another dimension to the use of 8mm film. He relates how a group of children using black leader film might scratch their original designs directly on the film and select background music for a most unusual audiovisual experience.

Mary Lou Ray discusses in her article entitled "Videotaping: You and Your Kids Can Do It" the procedures she used to teach television production to third grade students. She gives a number of success stories that illustrate ways elementary teachers have used the medium, provides steps to learning how to operate the equipment, and suggests activities to utilize television in the curriculum.

The final article in this section serves as a summation of the capabilities and creativity of elementary-aged children. Julius F. Schillinger, after working with inner-city children in Cleveland and American children in Germany, is firmly convinced that media belong to children. His students in Germany won a gift certificate in a photography contest and used the award to buy a movie camera. In his article he tells of some of their other projects and what he has learned from them.

STARTING OUT IN MEDIA PRODUCTION　　　　　Elise Wendel

Are you producing slide/tape shows either with students, staff, or on your own? If you are, I have suggestions you will find useful for improving your products; if you aren't, I offer encouragement and practical advice for starting out. During a big student project making a 240 slide/tape program, I was fortunate to have the help of a parent who is a photographer. Her expertise helped turn out a far more sophisticated product than I'd hoped for.

First, the students and I learned to "see" the photographs we were copying for our slides. We had been concentrating on subject matter. "We need a squirrel" — but the squirrel picture chosen might be too dark (only the brightest photos reproduce well with Kodak's Visualmaker), or too detailed (details tend to blur in reproduction). We learned how much composition of the original photo may or may not contribute to what we were trying to convey. A photo of children playing on a trash-littered beach is much more meaningful to our viewers than an empty trash-littered beach. From their comments, the students clearly showed that they were beginning to think about the more subtle aspects of their work.

Second, we learned what to do with imperfect slides. Many could be used in spite of sloppy margins, off-centered subjects, both easy mistakes to make with the Visualmaker. Photo supply houses carry slide mounts which are like mats for slides: they may be a small-centered square or circle, or two-small squares or circles in the same mat, or off-center squares or circles. Even an imperfect slide may contain enough to fill in one of these small mat spaces. With the bonus of using a slide which would otherwise have been discarded came a professional looking special effect. We emphasized a fierce lynx face or a delicate flower bud in this space. We learned the professional photographers' word for what we were making, "swipes": we were swiping photos published by photographers. This is legal, but only for educational, nonprofit purposes.

Starting a production requires a push from behind, I think. Many of us are comfortable with print and rationalize our reluctance with such excuses as, "I can't even take good pictures with an Instamatic" or "Children should read more, not fool with cameras." The photographic technique requirements are truly minimal — with lots of help available from Kodak's Visualmaker manual and their free loan slide/tape show on how to make visual presentations. The children really do read more as they research their project and write their script for the soundtrack complete with beeps for slide changes.

An excellent step-by-step guide for production is *Turning Kids On to Print Using Nonprint* by James L. Thomas (Libraries Unlimited, 1978); the author is methodical and thorough.

Reprinted by permission of the author and R. R. Bowker Company/A Xerox Corporation from *School Library Journal* 26 (November 1979):49.

For the district grant in which I was involved in producing the slide/tape show with twelve fourth to sixth graders, I received unanimous votes from the teachers on the grant committee. Teachers can be your push from behind, as they were mine, because although many would like to do this kind of project, they need help in order to accomplish their goals.

Now look at your situation. I think you can find a way to start your own media production.

YES, THEY CAN MAKE SLIDES, USE A DRY MOUNT PRESS, AND MORE

Robert T. Gasche

Could we teach kindergarten children certain techniques of media production that are often the sole domain of classroom teachers and media specialists? This question posed a unique challenge during the summer of 1974 and provided a most interesting fall quarter.

During preplanning, the possibility of starting a class-oriented media workshop was discussed with Julia Harper, one of our kindergarten teachers. She enthusiastically endorsed the idea and suggested an early start. Reflecting on some of the potential hazards, we became more and more dubious about involving children this young. We envisioned them having problems with such items as tacking irons, a dry mount press, and color lift materials. Nevertheless, we were game to try.

It was a somewhat apprehensive media person who rolled a cart of media materials to Mrs. Harper's kindergarten room at the P. K. Yonge Laboratory School at Gainesville, Florida, the first day of our project. Our schedule called for starting with the dry mount process, which entailed mounting pictures to construction paper with dry mount tissue.

The children were soon cutting out pictures from old magazines to mount on the multi-colored papers. As we showed them how to tack the dry mount tissue, with the tacking iron, to the back of the picture, trim and then tack to the construction paper, it became evident the children were quite capable of using the technique, with supervision, of course.

Oh, yes, fingers were burned—mine!!

The pupils quickly learned to use the dry mount press for the sealing of pictures to construction paper and they proudly put their names (some could write) on their finished product to indicate this personal accomplishment.

Mounting and Laminating

A follow-up activity was to laminate one of the dry mounted pictures. This technique of sealing the pictures in plastic posed more of a problem for the children; they had to learn to control the laminating film, tack it, trim corners, and seal in the hotter (270°) press. With help, they prevailed and soon learned that the plastic finish could be written on with chalk, grease pencil, or water color magic marker—and then erased.

Reprinted by permission of the author and the Association for Educational Communications and Technology from *Audiovisual Instruction* 21 (March 1976):60-61.

All through these media experiences the calm presence of Mrs. Harper helped to set the tone of enjoyment and learning. There was no question where the love, yet firmness when necessary, for these youngsters was centered.

In one incident, a child cut out a cigarette ad with a picture of a clock on it. Mrs. Harper was quick to pick up on this and asked the boy if he was sure he wanted that ad as his picture to laminate. When he answered, "Yes," she suggested that the slogan "It's time to stop smoking" be printed on his paper. This ability to relate so effectively with the children continued be be a strong influence on the success of the program.

Messy Is Best

The somewhat messy color lift process, with soak and wash solutions constantly in use, became one of the group's favorite media experiences. What a time they had, cutting out pictures to match the slide mounts and transparency frames, and sealing them with laminating film in the dry mount press. Squeals of glee were sometimes heard at the soaking pans as the colors became vividly apparent in the plastic sheets. They had to peel off the paper and rinse the color transparency in clear water to get the clay residue off the back of the plastic. After drying, they mounted the transparencies in slide mounts or regular size transparency frames and projected them on the screen. It really gave the children a thrill to see so clearly the results of their handiwork on a large screen.

Photograms in the Bathroom

In preparation for the making of photograms, Mrs. Harper had the pupils prepare small envelopes containing three or four objects and plastic letters that would spell their names. They placed these objects on photo-paper in the "darkroom," set up temporarily in the boys' bathroom, and proceeded to develop the prints.

To convert the bathroom a 25-watt red light bulb replaced the regular incandescent lamp; the window and door cracks were sealed with tape and construction paper. To produce a photogram, objects (leaves, cut outs, scissors, ruler, etc.) are placed on a piece of photographic paper, exposed to light for about three seconds and developed in the regular manner. Three trays were used—developer, stop bath, and fix. The basin was used to wash the prints for about a minute.

A short time on a drying table and the children had a permanent, personalized photogram. It didn't take long to make a bulletin board display of these prints for all to see and share.

Pictures on the Ceiling

By combining the use of a thermofax copier (most schools have one) with colored thermal transparencies and 35mm slide mounts, the children were able to produce their own color slides. To get an outline to work from, we traced the edges of several slide mounts on a spirit master and ran off enough Ditto copies for the group. The children then drew pictures with No. 2 pencils or black thin-line magic markers within the margin on the sheets of paper. Using this guide assured the pupils that what they drew could be projected as a slide.

When the drawings were completed (a series could be drawn) pupils placed a sheet of thermal transparency over the drawings and ran it through the copy machine. The results were a sheet of pictures fused into the plastic transparency. These pictures were then cut with scissors to fit the slide mount and an iron was used to seal them inside the cardboard frame.

A slide projector and screen were set up to show these slides. However, the children quickly learned they could get huge images by projecting on the ceiling and adjacent walls. The ensuing slide show was a treat!

Crayons and Spirit Masters

To help pupils learn design characteristics and create "instant patterns," we set up an art table and a drying table, and filled the sink half full of water (a dishpan or plastic tray will do as well).

A "flowing" kind of design was drawn on a spirit master by each pupil in the group. This caused a carbon tracing to be on the back of the sheet the design was drawn on. Using the carbon side of the paper the children drew with crayons around their original design leaving about ¼-inch margin on either side of the carbon line. Quick immersion in water caused the purple carbon to bleed into the paper where there was no wax from the crayons. A few minutes on the drying table and the pupil had produced an exciting purple-hued design, providing a new dimension to coloring with crayons.

Helping Hands

Kindergarten children not only can learn these techniques, but seem quite capable of teaching others the process almost as soon as they have achieved the skill. Helping relationships develop with the taught quickly becoming teacher.

Additional help for this workshop was received from student interns and a fifth grade pupil from another school. But most of all, it was Mrs. Harper's presence and caring that caused the children to get involved – and to learn. This media workshop was lots of work, plenty of fun, and most importantly, opened up new fields of discovery for young children.

STUDENT-PRODUCED MEDIA
THROUGH ORGANIZED CHAOS

Andd Ward Cipriano

To a visitor, the scene would appear unstructured, unorganized, and bedlamatic. Chaos seemed to reign in the second grade classroom that Friday afternoon. Magazine pictures—hundreds of them—were strewn carelessly over the carpet. Desks and chairs were pushed back against the walls, children were chattering, laughing, shouting, and hurrying back and forth. Chaotic? Yes. But the youngsters were learning, creating, and enjoying the activities.

A stream of children came up to me and asked endless questions—"Will you listen to my story?" "Can I use more than 12 pictures?" "Where's the paper?" "Where's the glue?" "I finished. What should I do next?"

Responding to questions and giving help, I felt like a leaf being swept along in a heavy wind. The momentum was there, all right. The children were engaged in an absorbing visual literacy project which they found thoroughly enjoyable. One shy-looking darkhaired little girl said to me at day's end, "This was one of the best afternoons I've ever had!"

The project was a simple one, designed for maximum success and enjoyment. And designed to be done at the student's own pace. It is always remarkable and exciting to witness a student's motivation if he or she is given freedom to operate within basic guidelines. Away with nonsense about everyone doing the same thing at exactly the same time and producing exactly the same results. And banish the thought that the student must reach certain standards set in advance by the teacher. In many cases, I find that when teacher standards are high but more relaxed than rigid, youngsters do much better work. Because they, too, are relaxed. And since they feel free to put themselves into the project, they generally give their best and exceed original teacher expectations.

And this is what happened that Friday afternoon in Joyce Jarvis' second grade class at the Henry Barnard School in Providence, Rhode Island. Students took charge of their own learning, and the result was a gleeful educational experience. The objective was that each student should improve creative storytelling skills by getting additional practice in storytelling. Specifically—given the necessary materials and equipment, the student will select at least 12 magazine pictures, sequence them, audiotape a creative story about them, and paste the pictures on a long strip of paper for later classroom showing on the opaque projector.

Each child was given a score or more of pre-cut magazine pictures from a large carton picture box; he or she arranged selected tearsheets on the carpet. As soon as his or her story was formulated, each youngster came over to the cassette recorder and taped a narrative. Interestingly enough, I taught only the first child to operate the equipment. Thereafter, a snowball effect occurred, with each new

Reprinted by permission of the author and the Association for Educational Communications and Technology from *Audiovisual Instruction* 19 (October 1974):16, 18.

child getting instructions from the previous speaker. There were no problems—no accidental erasure, no unwanted pauses, and excellent audio quality.

Almost everyone plunged eagerly into the picture-sequencing activity. Two children, however, had difficulty finding any pictures or even thinking of a topic for the story. One girl's problem was solved when a classmate volunteered some help by selecting the first few pictures. A boy's problem was solved by abandoning altogether the activity and substituting a simpler one. He was handed a set of Photo Story Discovery cards. This less complex task appealed to him. He readily arranged the pictures and was able to tape an interesting story.

Since the purpose of the visual literacy exercise was to learn and achieve success, positive results were sought. The two youngsters who were unable to meet the objectives were not punished or treated as failures; rather, they were regarded as learners who were not ready for this particular behavioral task. At the next visual literacy session, they will probably have more self-confidence and might well be ready for the picture-sequencing activity. An important element in the success of student-produced media is the attitude of acceptance that the teacher brings. To look for and find success is infinitely more important than to emphasize negativism and failure.

SUPER CINDERELLA –
FOURTH GRADERS PUT
FANTASY ON FILM

Hetty Cramer

Children in today's classrooms are media oriented. Their out-of-school world is, very often, dominated by television, movies, and visually pervasive messages. But in my fourth-grade class in the Rush-Henrietta School System of suburban Rochester, New York, the kids were given a chance to turn the tables and send rather then receive the media message. This group made its own sound-track movie: an original—very original, I might add—version of Cinderella.

I had introduced the class to creative dramatics several months before I decided to try filmmaking with them. We had done simple scene improvisations of real and imaginary commercials, role-playing of familiar adult-child situations, spontaneous interpretations of inanimate objects or absurd occurrences—all of which were aimed at stimulating the children's imaginations and freeing their powers of expression. The kids were enthusiastic, and early in the spring a small group of them drafted a script, their own version of the Cinderella fairy tale. During each day's session of unrestricted activity time, the group of playwrights rehearsed their play. Spinoff groups of kids began planning costumes, props, and scenery. "Cinderella" was infectious and kids clamored to take part: it was their own creation.

Let's Put Our Play On Film

Clearly, there was a major production in the making. It was at this time that I suggested the possibility of using visual media, super 8mm movie film. It was a perfect opportunity to give the kids a chance to make their own media production. They would see the process of production first-hand by really doing everything themselves and perhaps, at the same time, get an unprecedented glimpse of themselves and their own individual abilities.

While I acted as coordinator and guide, production arrangements proceeded: a film scenario was prepared, acting roles were assigned, a camera crew was assembled to draft a shooting script, and plans were set in motion for costumes, props, and scenery. Rehearsals were scheduled without disrupting class work.

We borrowed a super 8mm soundtrack movie camera, and the film crew was instructed in its use. We timed the actual filming, so that all members of the camera crew could take turns, and we set up strict rules about the care and use of the camera. The classroom's natural light was sufficient for the automatically adjusted camera and so we were able to do many types of simple shots—panning

Reprinted by permission of the Association for Educational Communications and Technology from *Audiovisual Instruction* 21 (March 1976):70-71.

and zooming interspersed with long and short straight shots of the actors — by standing either on a chair or on the floor with the hand-held camera.

One full afternoon was set aside for the filming. Everything went smoothly. However, we discovered that there was a lot of extraneous noise on the sound track, so we decided that we should do a voiceover. Using a projector that also records, the children repeated their lines while watching the film (which had been processed with a magnetic strip for recording). To my amazement, everyone remembered his or her part, word-for-word.

"Cinderella" generated cohesive spirit among the class; each person's responsibilities were vital in making a successful production. Everyone performed his or her task expeditiously and with relish. The student director needed only to sequence events within scenes, and on occasion she called for more expressive action. Beyond insights about organization, however, the children were learning about perception and communication. This movie-making experience fast became a remarkable educational adventure for all of us.

With novel contemporary treatment, the familiar fairy tale was transformed into a version that reflected the kids' own ideas about adults, themselves, and the world. The tempo raced along with hilarious events. This was a fantasy illuminated by reality.

The cast of characters included a beautiful but opportunistic stepmother, a king who discharged his queen (a lady nearly always appearing in hair rollers) for a younger model, a TV-addicted fairy godmother, a modern-day Cinderella who really didn't want to wear the glass slippers but preferred to dance barefoot, and a disoriented Snow White who hailed a cab to exit when she found she was in the wrong play. Two male commentators, reminiscent of TV sportscasters, acted as part-time narrators and part-time participants. A pause mid-way in the action gave the prince a chance to endorse a commercial product.

The kids were justifiably proud of their finished product and conducted an assembly so that parents and the kindergarten through sixth-grade classes could view the film.

What began as the experiment of a few grew into a project that involved us all. The filmmaking adventure had countless bonuses. The obvious were the children's improved speaking abilities and poise, their drive to work together to complete a project, their developing organizational abilities, and their desire to follow-through and improve on what they had done, as in the case of the voice-overs, for example. Yet the project took only about two weeks. We found we had time for everything: we did the basics and did our film too.

AVI talked to Hetty Cramer about her filmmaking project. Here are some excerpts from that exchange:

AVI: Many elementary school teachers use classroom dramatics, but is the additional element of movie-making possible for any teacher?

CRAMER: Yes, I think so. It had never been done before in the school where I was teaching, and many of the other teachers there became interested in the project.

AVI: What about less experienced teachers — can they tackle a project like this?

CRAMER: Yes, but I think more support from the faculty and administration would be necessary for them. With nine years of teaching experience, I was able to go ahead on my own.

AVI: Then you had done this sort of thing before?

CRAMER: Not exactly. I had made super 8mm movies but never a complete project working with young children. I had started a movie with youngsters at the Teachers College, Columbia University laboratory school, Agnes Russell. Using a super 8mm camera, my group of eight-year-olds filmed a documentary, "The Battle of Morningside Heights," on the site of that Revolutionary War battle which is located on the campus of Columbia University. But school closed before we were able to edit the footage. Nevertheless, it was a valuable experience for all of us.

Since then, I've done an audiotape dramatization of *Charlotte's Web* with eight-year-old boys. I didn't think they would be able to do the whole story, but they did.

AVI: Then children take naturally to working with media?

CRAMER: Oh yes. Much more so than adults realize. Children are used to television. All the teacher needs to do is coordinate and guide the production. The children do the rest.

AVI: Then filmmaking is within the ability of the average child?

CRAMER: Of course. In fact, one of our "Cinderella" camera crew was from the learning disabilities class. He enjoyed the project immensely and did very well. Everyone was working together — not competing — and he was able to participate without fear of failure.

AVI: What would you say are the most important results from such a project?

CRAMER: It makes a happier situation in the classroom. The children get a terrific feeling of accomplishment when they see themselves or their work on film and recognize their own abilities. I think this is very important. And they learn the value of cooperation and participation. Everyone's contribution is needed to make the film a success.

FILMMAKING IN THE CLASSROOM: SCRATCHING ON FILM

Ed Price

Almost everyone is familiar with the technique of painting on clear film with felt markers and India ink. There is, however, another technique of marking on film that is just as easy and less messy than painting. It involves scratching the black film with pins or other sharp implements and then running the result through a projector. All you need in your classroom are three inexpensive items: a length of black 16mm photo leader, pins and a roll of cellophane tape.

The black leader can be ordered from most custom film laboratories (such as Capitol Film Laboratories, Inc., 470 E St. S.W., Washington, D.C. 20024). Four hundred feet of this black photo leader will cost about $10-15 and will last the students several sessions.

When you order your black 16mm photo leader, remember to specify *photo leader* or you may end up with black plastic leader, which is no good for your purposes. After you receive the film, have the children tape their pins to the eraser end of their pencils and you're ready to go.

Allot each student a five-foot piece of film and let him scratch designs on the emulsion side of the film (the dull side). This will yield white scratches when projected.

As each child finishes scratching his piece of film, splice the sections together on a reel and show it on a projector. If you have 30 children in your room, their sections together yield about four minutes showing time at sound speed or about five-and-one-half minutes at silent speed, assuming your projector is equipped to run at 18 frames per second.

After the children view the film, ask them to select music to accompany their finished production. Fast music—bluegrass banjo, for example—is best.

When the music has been selected and the film is complete, show it to other classes in the school and have the children explain how the film was made. It just may start an epidemic of film-scratching throughout the building.

Reprinted from *Teacher* 91 (May/June 1974):30-31. Copyright © 1974 by Macmillan Professional Magazines. Used by Permission of The Instructor Publications, Inc.

VIDEOTAPING: YOU AND YOUR KIDS CAN DO IT

Mary Lou Ray

"Cut! Let's take it from the top." A Hollywood movie set or network TV studio? No. But they *are* the words of an experienced television performer—a third-grade boy playing a part in a television show being produced in his classroom.

Television production is an everyday occurrence in the Clarksdale, Mississippi, public school system. Robert Ellard, Clarksdale's superintendent of schools, who is constantly on the lookout for new ways to improve instruction, says, "Television is ... one of the most important tools we can use in helping our children."

Television is a part of life for today's children—by the time a child graduates from high school, he or she will have averaged 12,000 hours in school and 15,000 hours watching television. Several years ago, the Clarksdale schools began to capitalize on this interest by bringing television sets into the schools; student viewed instructional programs that were produced elsewhere.

Then two years ago, Mike Seymour, a former U.S. Army TV producer/director, was appointed television coordinator. Having seen the power of the medium as an instructional tool, Mr. Seymour is convinced that "television is probably the greatest technological advance for education." He believes that "it can become a tremendous extension of the teacher."

As soon as he began, Mr. Seymour started trying to interest teachers in videotaping various kinds of classroom activities. It was slow at first. Most teachers lacked confidence, but Mr. Seymour's enthusiasm and nonthreatening manner finally convinced a couple of teachers to give it a try.

He says, "Videotaping really isn't complicated. It takes about half an hour to show a teacher how the equipment works—to set up, record and play back the tape on a television monitor."

Mr. Seymour broadcast those first programs over the local cable TV channel. Kids and teachers could view them in schools during the day, and parents could watch them at home in the evening. The reaction was great. As you might guess, Mr. Seymour's days are rather frantic now, as he tries to respond to all requests for production and broadcast assistance.

What sort of programs are the elementary school teachers producing and what do they accomplish? Helen Hollomon, an intermediate level teacher at Oliver Elementary, says that one of her class's programs called, "To Soap or Not to Soap," had community-wide impact. The plot involves two boys who decide there are better things to do on Halloween than play tricks.

Ms. Hollomon's students adapted the program from a play script, added Halloween songs sung by a student chorus and made scenery and costumes.

Reprinted from *Teacher* 92 (January 1975):47-48, 106. Copyright © 1975 by Macmillan Professional Magazines. Used by permission of The Instructor Publications, Inc.

During the week preceding Halloween, the program was aired several times in school and at night.

"Afterwards," Ms. Hollomon says, "I got many calls praising our program for helping to cut down on vandalism."

In class there were other benefits as well. After the children saw programs they produced, Ms. Hollomon noticed general improvement in grammar and pronunciation and a recognition of the need to follow instructions.

When Joyce Aldridge, a sixth-grade teacher at Oakhurst, was presenting a unit on drug abuse, one of her students, Pamela Jones, asked if she could write a TV program. Pamela and her older sister read everything they could about drugs. Then they wrote the script.

Pamela and her classmates eagerly produced the show. Later Pamela said she felt great. "It isn't every day that a girl gets to see her script produced on television, and kids told me they learned a lot."

What about television production with younger children? Will it work? Sara Cannon, first-grade teacher at Oliver Elementary, knows it does. Last year her children enjoyed and learned from a vocabulary-building educational television series, *Words Are for Reading*, distributed by National Instructional Television. This year they are producing their own vocabulary game shows. Ms. Cannon finds that students are highly motivated to learn the lessons their classmates demonstrate on television. She says, "Videotaping encourages children to respond and act freely."

Mike Flynn sends his students out to tape interviews, field trips and special reports.

Now *You* Try It

Maybe the Clarksdale teachers have convinced you. Now what do you need to know to try videotaping in your classroom? (If your school doesn't already have the equipment, see [pages 70-71] for information on costs, etc.)

1. Corral whoever is in charge of equipment in your school and ask for a video lesson.

2. When you are set up for your first taping session with the children, remember that videotaping is basically a point and shoot operation. Just adjust the camera, as you were shown in your lesson, until the picture in the viewfinder is pleasing to your eye. That is all there is to it. Now start the recorder, aim the camera and you are videotaping!

3. Keep it simple to start with. Later you can try multiple actions, music, sound effects, etc.

4. Concentrate on the key action. As the cameraperson, you decide what the viewer will see. When you have some experience, you will find that older children can readily learn from you how to do the taping themselves.

5. With immediate playback you can look at what you have taped; if you don't like it, rewind and reshoot. All you have lost is a little time.

You will want to immediately play back all videotapes you make for the class to see. Suppose, after a few attempts, you make a tape that you and your students want others to see. How can you arrange this?

Here are several possibilities:

School viewing. Many schools have a central distribution system with all classrooms wired. A tape can be viewed over any or all TV monitors in the school at the same time. Or pass the tape around for viewing in individual classrooms.

School system viewing. Some schools are interconnected so that a tape can be shown throughout the system in all schools. Or, the tape can be duplicated for other schools.

Community viewing. Many cable companies provide a channel for educational use as in Clarksdale.

Videotaping Activities

Language Arts

After several sessions of creative writing, have your students choose their favorite story or book to dramatize as a television program. A remedial reading class in Thomastown, Mississippi, wrote a TV script based on the antics of *Amelia Bedelia* by Peggy Parish (Harper & Row; Scholastic, paperback) then taped it as a puppet show.

Mathematics

Many parents are unfamiliar with the metric system. When you conclude your study unit, encourage the children to create and tape for their parents a program illustrating the concepts and terms they have learned. If the program cannot be broadcast to the community in the evening, invite the parents to a "Metric Night" featuring it.

Interpersonal Relationships

The aim of this activity is to help children develop and increase their concern and respect for each person as an individual. Divide the class into small groups and ask each group to role play a certain situation that might occur in the classroom — tattling, ignoring the newcomer, cooperating in a game, teasing the poor reader, sharing with a friend, being a bully, turning in found money. Tape the dramas. As you play them back for the class, interesting and meaningful discussions will take place.

Persuasive Language

Here's a way to help children become critical thinkers, confident in their own ideas and judgments when confronted with the persuasive power of the printed and visual communications media. Have the children study the good and bad techniques of advertising: glittering generalities, the bandwagon approach, the straight pitch, the soft sell, the expert, the demonstration. Then create with the kids a product ahd have them produce and tape commercials for it, using the various techniques studied.

The children might also watch for and analyze different types of public service announcements—about drug abuse, pollution and smoking—and then try producing some of their own.

Year-end Review

In the spring, when children's thoughts are on everything except school, try a television game show modeled after the "G.E. College Bowl." Competitions can be planned within a classroom, between two classes in the school or between schools.

Videotaping is a different kind of teaching tool. But how do the children feel about it? Listen to some sixth-graders:

"It helps me learn better."
"I really get into it."
"Better than the teacher."
"It helps me pay attention."
"Everybody can see you."
"I feel like a teacher."
"You're doing something special."

Finally, from a girl who used a portable videotape camera to do a visual, rather than a written, report on trees: "It's better than copying a report out of a book." Amen!

Videotaping Equipment and Cost

The accompanying article describes the benefits that videotaping can bring to a classroom and some techniques to use with it. Many schools have all the equipment. Most have some of it—at least some TV monitors.

The following is a rundown of everything needed to provide a basic system, allowing for a full range of activities including viewing, videotaping and playback. The cost may sound high, but with school- and district-wide sharing, a few pieces of equipment can go a long way.

1. A 21-inch or larger color-TV monitor that meets specificatons for an in-classroom educational receiver (about $350). This monitor provides three kinds of viewing: tapes you make and play back; tapes you or others have recorded elsewhere; television programs broadcast over regular commercial and educational channels.

2. A rolling video cart ($40-100). This cart holds the TV monitor and the videocassette player/recorder. It isn't essential but makes the equipment easily portable.

3. A color videocassette player/recorder (about $1,500-1,800). Hooked up to the camera, this machine records what you are taping and then plays it back for viewing through the TV monitor. Additionally, it can play cassette tapes

recorded elsewhere and record and playback on-air TV programs. (The old reel-to-reel videotape recorders were mechanically complex, with many "dos and don'ts." The videocassette era has altered this by providing an "encapsulated tape." You simply drop the cassette into the machine and push the "record" and "play" buttons.)

4.   Video camera. Recent technical breakthroughs have resulted in easily operated, yet ruggedly built video cameras. About $800 buys a compact black and white camera, a tripod, microphone, cables, an electronic viewfinder, a zoom lens and a carrying case. Color cameras are considerably higher — $4,000 and up.

5.   In place of the player/recorder and camera, many schools are purchasing completely portable equipment. Carried and operated by one person, this battery-operated system consists of a hand-held video camera connected to a lightweight shoulder- or back-carried videotape recorder/player. It records picture and sound, plays back the tape on a monitor and records on-air TV programs ($1,800 and up for black and white — color is higher). — *M.L.R.*

MEDIA ARE TOOLS FOR CHILDREN   Julius F. Schillinger

I get an exhilarating feeling when I see the expressions on children's faces or hear their exclamations as the images on their first pictures begin to appear in the developing tray in the darkroom. And the frustration that children experience in trying to load, in complete darkness, their first roll of exposed negatives onto a film reel is, in retrospect, quite humorous. But it's just a matter of time before they become expert.

My experiences with children in media-related learning activities lead to one conclusion: media are tools for children. Using media gives them a chance to say who they are, where they are, how they think, and how they see the world.

They Teach Themselves

The images children capture with their cameras, for example, can become an entire story for them, complete with all the requisites for good storytelling. If the stories they compose from their pictures are then tape-recorded and written by them (or for them, in the case of very young children), they will begin to associate sounds with symbols, especially as they play back their recordings and hear their own voices pronouncing the words they see on paper.

For many children, the step from visual composition to reading and other language arts skills can be easy and self-generated. Thus, children begin to teach themselves — with media as their tools.

Creating Their Own Textbooks

One recent media-centered learning project, which I incorporated into an English curriculum, involved nine sixth-grade children at the John F. Kennedy School in West Berlin, Germany. During the course of the 1974-75 school year, children learned to use a simple Instamatic camera, more sophisticated 35mm and twin-lens-reflex cameras, both cassette and reel-to-reel tape recorders, a super 8mm movie camera, slide projectors, 16mm and super 8mm movie projectors, and the Kodak Ektagraphic Visualmaker (a simplified photographic copy stand that uses an Instamatic camera). In addition, the children learned to develop and print from their own black-and-white negatives in a photographic darkroom.

The youngsters used the media for several projects. For example, each child created a visual-verbal textbook — in effect, his or her own reading book, which became a photographic record of weekly experiences at home, at school, and in the community. Children made tape-recorded or written descriptions to accompany the pictures.

Reprinted by permission of the author and the Association for Educational Communications and Technology from *Audiovisual Instruction* 21 (March 1976):67-69.

In another instance, children used color slides or movies to accompany the lyrics of their favorite records. The children also planned, took, arranged, developed, and printed photographs and, sometimes, sequences that communicated an idea that they believed was relevant (e.g., the effects of overpopulation or the need to clean up the environment). By editing the finished slides and recording necessary dialogue and music onto tape, each child or group of children arranged a visual-verbal composition for presentation to the project class as well as to other classes, administrators, teachers, and parents.

With the media as their tools, they learned the various components of literature. They discovered that plot means a story has a beginning, goes somewhere, and has an ending. They had to decide the message — what they wanted to say; the mood — how the story made them feel; and the atmosphere — what kind of feeling they hoped to project to their audiences.

Peer Group Motivation

The children were tremendously gratified when their peer group audiences confirmed, by their reactions, that an idea was communicated. This left me with the impression that motivation in these types of projects comes from acceptance, not by the teacher, but by the peer group. One child in particular, who was considered "slow" by many teachers and students, did a two-month study of Australian bush tribesmen, and culminated his study with a fascinating, self-synchronized, slide-narrative-music presentation. When other children viewed the presentation, they were so moved, they heartily applauded and cheered for this child. It was an exceptionally meaningful interaction, especially for the child, but also for everyone involved.

"Destiny Control" — Key to Success

Through projects such as these, the children gained a measure of control over their learning environment — "destiny control," a factor the now historic Coleman report (Coleman, 1966) points to as the most important element in academic success. Moreover, by photographing their nonschool world, project children capitalized on the external experiences they brought to the classroom.

What About the Nonvisual Child?

Media-based projects like this one can be extremely successful, but a word of caution is necessary. Erickson's studies (Erickson, 1969) indicate that only about one-half the general population can benefit from visual stimuli and activities. It would be completely wrong to force a nonvisual child (a "haptic" child, according to Erickson) to participate in the visual learning aspects of media-related projects. By doing so, one may in fact inhibit the creative ability of that child just as one would inhibit creative ability by forcing a "visual" child to pay special attention to tactile impressions and activities.

The experience of one child in my project illustrates Erickson's point. This child did not take one photograph or movie sequence during the course of the project. He wrote and directed taped dramas and comedies, acted in other children's movies, and wrote poetry to accompany other children's photographs, but did not express himself through a visual medium, and was not forced to. He did derive some benefit from media-based learning projects, however, because these projects did involve a multitude of tactile and other nonvisual experiences.

Perhaps the lesson to be extracted from this is that the child, not the medium or its content, must be kept at the center of all learning activities. Recent research supports Erickson and indicates that children differ in the sense or senses (tactile, visual, aural, etc.) through which they learn best. Media-related learning activities can provide an alternative—for those children who need it—to the written and oral methods of learning so prevalent today.

From Passive to Active Learning

Media-centered learning projects have been instrumental in changing the emphasis of learning from the acquisition of knowledge to the learning of how to learn, from children's passive listening and memorizing to children using all their senses to manipulate materials, conceptualize ideas, and improve communication skills. By putting media materials in the hands of children, educators can capitalize on the inherent intellectual curiosity and learning potential each child is born with. Media allow the child to explore the external world and himself, and exploration is fundamental to the learning process.

References

Coleman, James S., "A Survey of the Lack of Availability of Equal Educational Opportunities for Individuals by Reason of Race, Color, Religion, or National Origin in Public Educational Institutions at All Levels in the United States," U.S. Government Printing Office, 1966, pp. 500-583.

Erickson, Richard C., "Visual-Haptic Attitude: Effect on Student Achievement in Reading." *Journal of Learning Disabilities*, May, 1969, Vol. 2, No. 5, pp. 21-25.

Evaluation of the Project

Although the approaches employed in measuring the effectiveness of the project may not meet the tests of statistical rigor, perhaps sharing the experience of my project in this article can provide some insight into the potential value of child-centered, media-based learning activities.

Children were pre- and posttested using the California Standard Achievement Test of Vocabulary, Reading, and Comprehensive Skills, and the Slosson Oral Reading Test, in an attempt to prove that they would show significant differences in language development compared to a similar (in age, sex, and academic achievement) pre- and posttested control group taught without the use of media-based strategy. It can be argued that experimenter bias and small sample size (the control group also numbered nine) influenced the positive project results, but my findings show that the experimental group exceeded the mean gain of the control group by 20.938 on the CAT. Six of the nine children in the experimental group achieved a one-and-one-half to three-year growth in oral vocabulary while only two out of nine in the control group achieved similar growth. Significance could not be determined because of the small sample size.

V

VISUAL LITERACY PROGRAMS

When students look at the world around them what is it they see? Are they able to comprehend and interpret the meaning of the visual objects that constantly bombard them? To help students understand visuals, a variety of visual literacy programs across the curriculum have been established to develop visual competencies along with other sensory awareness.

The lead article in this section by M. Jean Greenlaw provides the reader with two definitions of visual literacy along with what the author proposes to be the difference between "seeing" and "visualizing." Greenlaw briefly traces the movement toward developing awareness of the importance of visual literacy and then shows how educators might promote such a program using the most commonly available medium — books. Suggestions for combining books and nonprint are also discussed.

Annelle S. Houk and Carlotta Bogart maintain in their article how essential the exploration of visual literacy skills are to the total communication development of elementary children. The authors explain that teachers who want to provide their students with the skills necessary to be visually literate "must help children explore what the children themselves perceive and how and why they perceive it" and not supply pat answers that the adult knows to be correct. They list steps to take as an adult in setting up the proper exploration process and discuss activities that will enable children to learn in a nonthreatening, creative atmosphere.

Roy Ferguson in "Seeing Sequentially: A Curriculum" describes the ways in which the Milford, Ohio schools are making their youngsters visually literate. An entire curriculum has been designed for children in grades one through twelve that, as Ferguson points out, will provide "visual communication skills which they need to live effectively in contemporary American society." Examples of what media are being used on each grade level are mentioned.

The last two articles in this section are exercises that might be tried by the reader in a group situation or with an individual student. "Fostering Visual Literacy: A Fun Exercise" by Roy E. Toothaker contains a listing of questions for interpretation and discussion with accompanying activities for four different pictures illustrating the Mother Goose rhyme, "Simple Simon." Toothaker has included a chart of comparison and contrast for the four illustrations that might be helpful for the reader in pointing out the differences. A bibliography of other useful Mother Goose rhyme books is given for future reference. "Little Red Riding Hood," illustrated by Nancy Earle, is a unique visual experience for young and old alike. Children might benefit from having this shared with a minimum of oral interpretation while they simply view the pictures. Once they have discussed the story arrangement as revealed in the pictures, they might want to recreate their own favorite story using only visuals to carry the message.

VISUAL LITERACY AND READING INSTRUCTION: FROM BOOKS TO MEDIA AND BACK TO BOOKS

M. Jean Greenlaw

"I've read that book twenty times and never seen what you just showed us!" This is a comment typical of graduate students enrolled in a reading materials class when they are first exposed to the concept of visual literacy. They have read or "seen" the material many times, but have not had training in extracting all the images that are embedded in the book. This is why there is need for the development of visual literacy. It enhances a visual experience by allowing us to obtain more than a surface reaction.

In an attempt to find a definition of visual literacy, a search of the literature revealed two. The members of the National Conference on Visual Literacy have agreed on the following definition:

> Visual literacy refers to a group of vision-competencies a human being can develop by seeing and at the same time having and integrating other sensory experiences. The development of these competencies is fundamental to normal human learning. When developed, they enable a visually literate person to discriminate and interpret the visible actions, objects, and symbols natural or man-made, that he encounters in his environment. Through the creative use of these competencies, he is able to communicate with others. Through the appreciative use of these competencies, he is able to comprehend and enjoy the masterworks of visual communications. (Fransecky and Ferguson 1973, p. 45)

Ross (1972) suggested that visual literacy is, " ... numerous techniques used by people to communicate with each other in non-verbal ways." It would seem that many advocate the teaching of visual literacy, but few have defined it in workable terms.

I propose that there is a difference between seeing and visualizing. When we "see" we respond to the surface patterns, but when we "visualize" we bring meaning to the image and react in a critical manner. Visually literate people, then, are those who have acquired the ability to make viable judgements about the images they perceive.

Development of Programs in Visual Literacy

A movement toward developing awareness of the importance of visual literacy has been obvious in the past five years. Though the concept has

Reprinted by permission of the author and *Language Arts* 53 (October 1976):786-90.

undoubtedly been with us much longer, the organized devising of programs has been recent.

An indication of increased interest in visual literacy is the proliferation of articles in educational journals. The entire May 1972 issue of *Audiovisual Instruction* was devoted to visual literacy and articles by Tanzman (1972) and Fillion (1973) have appeared in other journals.

Articles concerning schools that are involved in visual literacy projects are also increasing in number. Fransecky and Ferguson (1973) report on the Milford Project in a three-article series that gives specific guidelines for developing a visual literacy curriculum. Van Holt (1972) and Ferguson (1972) also summarize information on schools that have actively pursued visual literacy instruction.

A review of these articles reveals that many techniques have been used in an attempt to develop visual literacy in children. Films, both 16 mm and super 8 mm single concept loops, have been created by students. Slides, prints, filmstrips made on u-film, painting, dramatics, and interpretation of body language, have all been components of instructional programs. One element has been missing, however. It is an element available in almost every school which requires little or no additional outlay of money.

The Use of Books to Develop Visual Literacy

Books are familiar objects in a school, which teachers are accustomed to using. Therefore, with a modicum of additional experience and insight a teacher can become an advocate of visual literacy through a medium that is well-known and secure. Often, when awakened to the possibilities existent in visualizing a book, teachers become adept at sharing this knowledge with students, because it is exciting to find a new dimension in an old medium. Additionally, when students become aware of visualizing, their curiosity often leads them to scrutinize each picture book for the possibilities of embedded images. Picture books can be used at any level as a valuable tool to teach visual literacy.

The following are books that can be incorporated in a visual literacy study. Each has a dimension that goes beyond "seeing" and requires "visualizing."

On a superficial, but highly enjoyable level, Ellen Raskin has shown us that we often fail to see what occurs in our world. In *Nothing Ever Happens on My Block*, Chester Filbert sits on a curb and laments the lack of excitement in his life. As the reader can plainly see, all manner of action is taking place behind the child, but he is not even a seer. Pat Hutchin's *Rosie's Walk* depicts the same type of situation. Rosie the hen goes for a walk and is followed by a fox she never sees. She gets back in time for dinner, never knowing how many narrow escapes she incurred. These books make an obvious point, and can be used as a starter in the process of developing visual literacy.

Raskin's book *Spectacles* can be employed to show that things are not always what they seem. What looks to be a fire-breathing dragon knocking at the door is merely Great-aunt Fanny. And, the fuzzy green caterpillar in school turns out to be only a group of children. It is astounding what spectacles can do for seeing. Children can be lead to imagine what wondrous creatures can be created from ordinary pictures.

Some books tell two stories at once. Many people read the following two books and see but one story. *Rain Makes Applesauce*, by Julian Scheer, is a delightful nonsense tale with the recurring phrase "rain makes applesauce." What many readers fail to notice is that embedded in the nonsense pictures is a realistic tale that shows two children buying apple seeds, planting them, nurturing the tree, and finally getting applesauce from the apples. Blair Lent's Caldecott Award winning *The Funny Little Woman*, uses the same technique of telling two stories. The color pictures show what is happening to the funny little woman. But life goes on beyond her. Line drawings tell the story of what happens in the real world while she is in the land of the "oni's." Both worlds begin and end together, but there is a tale in the separation.

Those who are capable of visualizing will find devices used by some authors to add a dimension to their stories. Gerald McDermott uses a rainbow throughout *Arrow to the Sun* to symbolize the Pueblo Indian path of life. Jacob Lawrence employs a star in *Harriet and the Promised Land*, to show evidence of Harriet Tubman's destiny to lead her people to freedom. The star is present at her birth and then disappears. It reappears when she learns of the promised land, and recedes again until she is ready to lead her people out of slavery. From that point it is present in every picture portraying her flight. Clement Hurd's medium is woodcuts in *The Day the Sun Danced*; those depicting winter are distinct and harsh while a softer wash is used to convey the changes of spring.

There are many textless picture books which can serve as a stimulus for visual literacy and for many language experiences. *The Magic Stick*, by Kjell Ringi, is an example of a book of this type. "Once upon a time there was a stick. A boy found the stick and it was magic. Because of the stick the boy became many things." These words were supplied by fifth graders, but the story can be different each time, depending on how the reader visualizes the page.

These are a few examples of books that can be part of the development of visual literacy. Taking a step beyond books leads one into the realm of media.

Combining Books and Media

A creatively conceived book by Tana Hoban can be the step into media for students and teachers. *Look Again* shows us a very small part of a picture, framed in white. We then turn the page and see the picture in its entirety. The next page takes us one step further by placing the object in a larger context (e.g., swirls, a conch shell, and a child listening to the shell). Some of the initial pictures are easily identified, but others require visualizing in its strictest sense.

Once children have been exposed to the idea of *Look Again*, it is an easy step to creating their own books from magazine pictures or photographs they have taken. They will soon discover the intricacies of such a task. The process, itself, will involve increased use of visual literacy. The same idea could be pursued through film, if the equipment were available.

A study of story construction can also be a combined media/book undertaking. Story development can be beautifully shown in Maurice Sendak's *Where the Wild Things Are*. Sendak combines words, color and picture proportion to create a unified effect in this story. The book opens with Max making mischief. Text is on one page opposed by a small, drab picture centered in a frame of white. As the action rises the pictures get larger and brighter. They soon fill the page, bleed over to the next page, become double page spreads with less and less text at the bottom, until the climax is reached and there are three double pages of bold pictures entirely filling the space and no text present. The story comes to an end by reversing the pictorial process and ending with five words and no picture. The text is an integral part of the process as it builds and reverses in the same pattern as the pictures.

From *Where the Wild Things Are* one could move to a study of television form. What is the construction of various programs: soap operas, mysteries, cartoons, comedies, westerns, and news programs? What are the similarities and differences in comparison to books? What purpose do commercials serve? A comparison of television and book form might lead more students back to books.

Film could be studied in the same manner. There is probably more freedom in film than in television and the reasons for this could serve as a basis for an interesting class debate.

Another activity is to compare the same story produced in film and book. Gerald McDermott has created three films that are also available as books: *Arrow to the Sun, Anansi the Spider*, and *The Stonecutter.* Each is the same basic story in film and book, but the execution of each is quite different. The possibilities for development of visual literacy skills are enormous.

Color also provides a topic for study. Why do paperback book publishers produce the same title in different colors? They must be aware that color affects choice and serves as an attention-getting device. Have you ever watched someone trying to decide what copy of *Future Shock* to buy? The content is the same but the covers are available in blue, green, orange, and red. Which would you buy? Why? Students can easily find other examples of paperbacks with different colored covers. The question to pursue is—why?

Transfer this question of color to television and film. Why has there been increased sale of color TV's in comparison to black and white sets? Why are all television shows produced in color today? Why are some films being shot in black and white, rather than color? Given the choice, would you rather take color pictures or black and white? Why?

And Back to Books?

Actually, I have never left books. In our rush to be "in," to be "mod," to jump on the bandwagon, teachers have overlooked the possibilities of using books in conjunction with media to broaden and intensify the skills of visual literacy. Certainly, we should make better use of media in the classroom, but we do not need to exclude books in the process.

The teacher who makes use of all available sources of study and encourages students to integrate their learning, is the teacher who does not respond to fads but uses sound teaching principles. We must make more intelligent use of media in learning, because this is a media world. Students need to learn how to respond critically to the media that surround them in their daily lives. We must see that books are a part of the training to develop a visually literate populace.

References

Adult

Audiovisual Instruction (May 1972).

Ferguson, Roy. "Seeing Sequentially: A Curriculum." *Audiovisual Instruction* (May 1972): 16-18.

Fillion, Bryant. "Visual Literacy." *Clearing House* 47 (1973):308-311.

Fransecky, Roger B. and Ferguson, Roy. "New Ways of Seeing: The Milford Visual Communications Project." *Audiovisual Instruction* (April 1973): 44-49; (May 1973):56-65; (June 1973):47-49.

Ross, Samuel B., Jr. "Visual Literacy—A New Concept?" *Audiovisual Instruction* (May 1972):12-15.

Tanzman, Jack. "The Meaning and Importance of Visual Literacy." *School Management* 16 (1972):41.

Toffler, Alvin. *Future Shock*. New York: Bantam, 1971.

Van Holt, Jay M. "Visual Literacy: A Valuable Communications Tool." *Instructor* (Aug./Sept. 1972):130-132.

Child

Hoban, Tana. *Look Again*. New York: Macmillan, 1971.

Hurd, Edith Thacher. *The Day the Sun Danced*. Illustrated by Clement Hurd. New York: Harper & Row, 1965.

Hutchins, Pat. *Rosie's Walk*. New York: Macmillan, 1968.

Lawrence, Jacob. *Harriet and the Promised Land*. New York: Simon & Schuster, 1968.

McDermott, Gerald. *Anansi the Spider*. New York: Holt, 1972.

_____. *Arrow to the Sun*. New York: Viking, 1974.

_____. *The Stonecutter*. New York: Viking, 1975.

Mosel, Arlene. *The Funny Little Woman*. Illustrated by Blair Lent. New York: E. P. Dutton, 1972.

Raskin, Ellen. *Nothing Ever Happens On My Block*. New York: Atheneum, 1966.

_____. *Spectacles*. New York: Atheneum, 1968.

Ringi, Kjell. *The Magic Stick*. New York: Harper & Row, 1968.

Scheer, Julian. *Rain Makes Applesauce*. Illustrated by Marvin Bileck. New York: Holiday House, 1964.

Sendak, Maurice. *Where the Wild Things Are*. New York: Harper & Row, 1963.

WHAT YOU SEE'S NOT ALL YOU GET

Annelle S. Houk and Carlotta Bogart

Especially in the elementary school, what children need for their development of visual literacy is not instruction in viewing but guidance in the process of discovering what, how, and why they see. Because adults are better at analyzing, sequencing, and unifying, we can help today's visually alert children bring to conscious control what they have already perceived. They may out-see us, but they are not yet mature enough to think soundly totally without help.

The less aware Larry is of either the specific content or the meaning of what he has seen, the more he will lack both the vocabulary and the skill to communicate. Therefore a major problem between adults and children in elementary school is first understanding and then expanding the children's translations of visual experience into words. The teacher who wants to lead young children toward visual literacy—and eventually to reading and writing skills—must help children explore what the children themselves perceive and how and why they perceive it. However, that exploration requires infinite patience and skillful avoidance of the least suggestion by the teacher that there are correct answers that adults already know and that the children must get right.

From an adult point of view this exploration of the child's visual learning processes involves three steps. First, awareness of visual detail requires John's development of a precise vocabulary for the concrete, including synonyms, rooted soundly in the child's own personal experience. This is not a list a teacher can provide. Second, the child, by recognizing his intensely personal context and attempting to share it, learns to pick out what is universal, hence communicable. Third, analyzing how he perceives something—what senses are coordinated from what cues—prepares him to think for himself in an orderly fashion that gives him intellectual command over his experience instead of leaving him emotionally subject to it.

Visual-verbal games are activities that permit children to learn without threat. Games are not graded. Errors are as welcome as accuracy and a lot more fun because they permit play with the absurd. Besides, play commands much greater attention and involvement from the child than work does; and each child brings his or her real self to play while children often bring to work what they think adults want.

The word *game* suggests a structure, but the structure of visual-verbal games is in the nature of the thing explored, not in an external rule system. Nor is this a game that has a single exit from a preplanned route that one player races other contestants to reach so that he can "win." Neither is there a "product" in the sense that there is when a project or an activity is completed. And there is no objective way to know which child has contributed or gained most—hence earned an "A."

Reprinted by permission of the authors and *Elementary English* 51 (March 1974):445-48.

When a whole group plays verbal games, children can make a contribution at their own level of maturity and from their own particular kind of perception. For example, the most visual and most verbal children usually can contribute a wider variety of vocabulary. They are natural classifiers and natural collectors of synonyms. But the psychomotor child, who often reads poorly and sometimes has a limited vocabulary of synonyms, will excel in contributing purposes and functions of things that the nonmanipulating observer often cannot see. Therefore, every child both contributes to and benefits from verbal play with the visual.

Nor are visual-verbal games the poor man's means to visual literacy—a substitute for cameras and film study in schools financially unable to afford them. No matter how rich or poor a school is in visual equipment and materials, what matters most to the development of each child's mind is what goes on in his or her own head. Certainly, physical manipulation of actual pictures in Tom's hand or in his camera is desirable help for a child developing mental images—visual symbols—that he can then manipulate with or without the presence of the object symbolized. This manipulation of visual symbols in the mind is now virtually universally agreed to be a prerequisite for the oral, written, or read use of words. In other words, an adequate store of visual symbols that can be translated into oral verbal symbols is necessary for any child who is to learn to read or to learn to read well. Visual-verbal games are concerned with that internal symbolic play—though the play may be stimulated by external visuals like objects, photographs, films, and lights.

The objective of a visual-verbal game is the unification of a whole group's experience with the recognition that nevertheless each individual's learning from a particular game also will be unique. In a successful visual-verbal game, everyone wins a better command of vision, vocabulary, and participation in socializing activity.

Any concept is good ground for such games, and any visual source of information from a magazine cover to a brick to a film can be the subject for such play. Games that begin with the object (say the brick) begin with the identification of details of size, shape, color, texture [recognition]. Everyone can contribute at least a crack or a corner, and every piece of concrete information leads to a "why" [recall]. Why is it red? Why rectangular? Why hard? Why did it crack? The third step of most visual-verbal games that begin with an object is "what is it for?" [application]. As children draw from experience, they add to the experience and vocabulary of others. And every child unifies experience partially by the act of making it verbal.

Games that derive from a concept must begin and proceed in much the same way. By sharing experience in enough detail, children in a group arrive at a concept level with enough shared information and understanding that no one whose initial experience might have been more limited is forced to feel inferior. Nor will initial cultural differences exclude anyone from play.

For the purpose of exploring the concept of analogy, for example, suppose again that the game begins with a brick. Children still need a conscious knowledge of the concrete qualities of the brick, of its formation, and of its uses before they can make contrasts or comparisons of it with other things. Once sure of a wide base of shared experience, an adult can lead the children to name things that are like bricks. Since those things are not physically present as the brick is, they require both visual and verbal imagination—imagination also rooted, however, in individual experience. When such play is really free, a remarkable sophistication of information will emerge even from very young children. Someone will know how concrete blocks are made, and someone will verbalize the fact that blocks and bricks are man-made is a similarity.

But they will know differences as well. Someone, for example, may know that making brick requires heating natural materials and making concrete blocks requires drying of a man-made mixture. Then someone will undoubtedly say that rocks are like bricks in their uses and in other ways but are not manmade. Someone least expected may volunteer why the rocks vary so much in shape and in substance. And a child who has shown least evidence of either an organized interest or a creative spark will turn out to have a rock collection and the whole class will have to look at it the next day.

There are no concepts important to the education of children that cannot be approached through visual-verbal games.

One of the most frustrating concepts to approach early by direct instruction, however, is that of modification. Yet, even very young children will play drawing games that illustrate the principle clearly. One child names a concrete object—*boy*. Another draws a boy on the chalkboard. A third suggests *tall*. A fourth changes the picture on the board to fit. A fifth says *fat*. A sixth changes the figure on the board. A seventh says *green*. The more absurd and extreme the modification and the worse the drawing, the more the fun—and the more permanent and personal the learning.

The same translation of changes can be demonstrated by an actor given instructions by his friends: "Walk." "Faster." "Much faster." Again, to make the learning most permanent, the whole group should participate in explaining both what kinds of changes are required and why. And the less verbal children should be encouraged to be actors as well as instructors.

Translation can itself be played. For example, ask a child to name something living. Suppose the answer is "tree." The group can then decide how it wishes to change the tree: grow it, cut it, have it die of disease or fall from a storm. Whatever the choice, in each change, the group can determine what of the original is kept, what is changed, and how. Soon the group will be translating *tree* into *sawdust* or *table* or *telephone pole* or *firewood*—even *smoke*—without knowing that they are working at one of the most difficult concepts we attempt to teach.

Again, visual-verbal games permit translation of actions as easily as of objects. Suppose a game begins again with "walk." The group quickly will define the action, recognize the requirement of legs, and limit walking to animals and machines made in imitation of animals. Once the concept of walking has been explored to the point of understanding its three components—the walker, the mechanism for walking, and the medium walking requires—translation can continue. Now change any one of the three components, for example, the man to a rock. The group will change *walk* to *roll* or *fall* because they will remove the legs visually and verbally. But they will not change the ground required for the motion. If the ground is made into *air* (a change of the medium), the children will immediately translate legs into wings and walking into flying—with considerable fun if legs rather than arms are replaced with wings. A change of the mechanism—for example from *leg* to *oar*—will cause children to explore motions in water, and they will come up with analagous mechanisms like *duck feet, fish fins*, and even *Mark Spitz*.

Obviously, visual-verbal games are time-consuming, poorly organized, and disruptive not only of that day's plans but perhaps of those for next week.

Nevertheless, if a check of concepts or content is made at some distance from the playing of a game, recognition stays high, recall is good, and vocabulary remains expanded. Furthermore, any reading or study in any segment of knowledge even remotely related to a successful former game will be pounced on with enthusiasm and cross-referenced to the game.

Such games encourage responses that are spontaneous, but they are not at all so random as they seem. The concept or the visual object has an inherent unity that both provokes diversity and sets limits. Those unified opposites are the substance of all definition and classification, the root of both logic and language. Short of verbal and logical command, visual experience exercises emotional control over mind. If visual literacy is to be more than an elitist fad on the one hand and an avoidance of the difficult problem of keeping reading alive for the majority of students on the other, it must lead to growth of the mind to a productive and creative level. Such a level of mental control has been expressed only by disciplined art. Since the word must remain the highest potential medium of expression for most of our children—with few becoming creators of music or film or other nonverbal art—visual-verbal games are serious play.

SEEING SEQUENTIALLY:
A CURRICULUM

Roy Ferguson

If you are a citizen of Milford, Ohio, chances are that one of these days you'll look out the window and discover a small child with a camera taking pictures of the cement rectangles on your sidewalk and the wooden triangles in the eaves of your house.

Later, on your way to the store you might find yourself in a "walk-in" role as part of a film being shot by a group of high school students at the shopping center.

If you asked one of the students what was going on he would explain that he was part of a visual communications program developed by teachers in the Milford schools to help students become visually literate.

And if your curiosity were aroused enough to investigate what this visual communications program was all about, you would discover that teachers and students at all levels in the school system were busy designing and implementing learning activities to develop the visual skills indispensable to effective living in an age of multi-media communications.

Cameras in hand, first graders are out in the town discovering and photographing the shapes — circles, squares, triangles, rectangles — which form their environment. In their classrooms these students are learning the importance of clear communication as they discover how body language works.

They listen to a tape recording of a loud train whistle and a distant voice; and as they draw what they hear, the children begin to discover the relationships between sounds and images. Later, when the students share their photographs of environmental shapes, they will see that the form which things are given often implies meaning. Their teacher will use these same pictures to introduce a study of elementary geometry later in the year.

A class of second graders is boarding as bus for a not-so-ordinary field trip to the zoo. They plan to bring the animals back to school ... captured on film ... and to make this field trip last the year round.

In groups (four to a camera), they will set out, some to take black-and-white photographs of the animals, others to record the entire trip on color slides. When the photographs have been processed, the children will talk about them to teacher's aides who will record the children's descriptions in visual-verbal reading books "written" by the children themselves. Chances are that all 16 books will be read several times by each student — and maybe the development of reading skills will be a bit easier for the children in this second grade class.

The students who took the slides will produce a slide-tape set which describes the trip. They will write the script, edit and sequence the slides, and narrate the

Reprinted by permission of the author and the Association for Educational Communications and Technology from *Audiovisual Instruction* 17 (May 1972):16-18.

sound track. Student artists will draw the title and credits and will photograph them with a visual maker.

The finished project, which will be shown to other students and to parents, will represent a complete communications experience using each of the five language arts—reading, writing, speaking, listening, and seeing.

Soon, some of the children will be talking about writing visual-verbal science books featuring their zoo pictures. The teacher will discover that the children's pictures can be used to begin a study of mammals. There will be talk about mounting an advertising campaign to persuade others to visit the zoo.

On the blackboard of a third grade classroom a series of student photographs showing how to fix a flat tire and another showing how to bake bread illustrate student understanding of how the camera can be used to communicate a process. The students in this class are clustered around a videotape recorder deciding the distance and angle of various shots as they plan to use the television camera to tell a story. After they have videotaped their pantomime, they will evaluate the production to determine if it represents clear and effective visual communication.

Similar evaluations are taking place up the hall as fifth grade students sequence a series of slides taken in the school. They are editing and sequencing the slides to tell the story of a classroom incident in which a student prankster is sent to the principal's office. When the slides have been edited and sequenced, the students will add a sound track of their own making.

A special film prepared especially for the visual communications project by WCPO Television, Cincinnati, is being intently watched by students in a sixth grade classroom. Featuring a WCPO news cameraman and a Milford student, the film explains how a news story is photographed for television. Students are reinforcing their awareness that visual communication involves conscious choice making and effective use of camera distance and angle. And they are discovering new visual communication devices such as subjective camera and zoom which they will use in a more sophisticated study of television and film in secondary school.

In the junior high school, eighth grade students are viewing television commercials as they explore techniques of visual persuasion and advertising. In the tenth grade these students will experience a learning unit in which they will study the more complicated aspects of film production.

A study of television and film documentaries will help high school juniors develop the seeing skills so important in the accurate perception and interpretation of the important events and ideas transmitted to them each day via the electronic communications media.

Perhaps as high school seniors, some of these students will make a film which sets forth their interpretations of life; or they might film a documentary which describes life in their own community.

No question about it—if you are a citizen of Milford, Ohio, you'll probably run into some kids with cameras one of these days. When you do, remember that those kids are involved in an educational program bound to have an important, positive effect on their lives. They are developing the visual communications skills which they need to live effectively in contemporary American society; they are becoming visually literate.

FOSTERING VISUAL LITERACY: A FUN EXERCISE

Roy E. Toothaker

This experience, designed to develop visual literacy, can be used with primary grade children through adults. Questions for discussion, for interpretation, and suggested activities may be used as the maturity of the participants warrants.

The illustrations of the well-known first stanza of the Mother Goose rhyme "Simple Simon" were done by four talented and experienced artists from the Chicago area. Each artist—Lois Axeman, Seymour Fleishman, Jerry Warshaw, and Ginny Linville Winter—has had wide experience in illustrating both trade books and textbooks.

> *"Simple Simon met a pieman,*
> *Going to the fair.*
> *Said Simple Simon to the pieman,*
> *'Let me taste your ware'."*

For Interpretation

- What do you think each character is thinking about?

- How old do you think Simon is in each one?

- What kinds of pies do you think each are?

- What does each illustrator leave to your imagination?

- What style or tone do you think each illustration conveys? Which are formal or informal? Old-fashioned or modern/contemporary? Traditional or nontraditional? Personal or impersonal?

- Which one would appeal *most* to pre-school children? To primary-grade children? To upper-elementary-age children? To early teenagers? To later teen-agers? To adults? Which one would appeal *least* to each of the above age groups?

For Discussion

- What is the center of attention in each illustration? How is the viewer's attention directed there? (Consider the placement, the

Reprinted by permission of the author from *Arts and Activities* 85 (June 1979):52-54, 65.

gaze, and the hands of the characters; consider the use of lines; consider the number and size of the pies.)

- How did each illustrator convey Simon's simpleness?

- To which of the senses (seeing, smelling, touching, tasting, moving) does each illustration appeal? How does each illustrator appeal to those senses?

- What general impression does each illustration give you?

Suggested Activities

- Compare and contrast the four illustrations. Consider *point of view, background, use of color, use of white space, use of line, use of form and shape, head coverings of the characters* (see accompanying chart for possible responses). You might, in addition, want to consider *the number of pies, the position of the pies in the illustration, how the pies are displayed, how the aroma is pictured, the feet and the legs of the characters*, and the like.

- Find and look at other illustrations of "Simple Simon." Find and look at illustrations of other nursery rhymes. There are several picturebook versions of nursery rhymes and specific nursery rhymes have been set to music in collections of songs, which have accompanying illustrations. Check your public or school library.

- Illustrate the same stanza of "Simple Simon" and compare yours with those of your classmates and with these four illustrations.

- Illustrate another stanza of the Simple Simon rhyme.

- Illustrate a scene (or stanza) from another nursery rhyme.

Bibliography

Many useful Mother Goose and nursery rhyme books are available. Among the many are the following picture books which have excellent illustrations and contain various versions of "Simple Simon."

The Tall Book of Mother Goose. Illus. by Feodor Rojankovsky. Harper & Row, 1942, by Western Publishing Co. 7 stanzas, pages 28-29.

The Mother Goose Treasury. Illus. by Raymond Briggs. Coward-McCann, 1966. 10 stanzas, pages 34-35.

Frank Baber's Mother Goose Nursery Rhymes. Illus. by Frank Baber. Gramercy Publishing Co., (Div. of Crown Publishers), 1976. 4 stanzas, page 113.

Mother Goose Rhymes. Illus. by Margot Austin. Platt & Munk, 1940. 2 stanzas, page 23.

Mother Goose. Illus. by Gyo Fujikawa. Grosset & Dunlap, 1968. 5 stanzas, page 22.

The Mother Goose Book. Illus. by Alice and Martin Provensen. Random House, 1976. 1 stanza, page 22.

Marguerite de Angeli's Book of Nursery and Mother Goose Rhymes. Illus. by Marguerite de Angeli. Doubleday and Co., 1954. 5 stanzas, pages 118-119.

Mother Goose and Nursery Rhymes. Wood engravings by Philip Reed. Atheneum, 1966. 8 stanzas, pages 16-18.

Brian Wildsmith's Mother Goose: A Collection of Nursery Rhymes. Illus. by Brian Wildsmith. Franklin Watts, 1970. 4 stanzas in one, page 55.

Mother Goose. Illus. by Tenggren. Little, Brown, 1940. 7 stanzas, page 54. (No illustration of Simple Simon but other full-color, full-page, "charming" illustrations of other rhymes such as, "Georgie Porgie," "Mistress Mary," "Peter, Peter, Pumpkin Eater," "Three Wise Men of Gotham," and an ideal one of "Jack Sprat.")

[*See* Chart of Comparison and Contrast and illustrations on following pages.]

Chart of Comparison and Contrast

Area to Consider \ Artist	Seymour Fleishman	Ginny Winter	Jerry Warshaw	Lois Axeman
Point of View	Close-up of upper front parts of bodies, Pieman in profile, front view of Simon	Almost perfect side views of complete bodies of both Pieman and Simon	Full view of front of Pieperson/ machine; Simon has his head toward Pieperson	Complete fronts of bodies of both characters in full view, faces in profile
Background	White space between Pieman and Simon is filled-in with color	None; there is plenty of empty white space	Bare minimum: two signs on narrow pole, some small dots	Complete, with a dirt road with its ruts and pebbles; blue sky and white billowy clouds; tents with pennants, in upper-right distance
Use of Color	Pastels, more subdued blue, green, black, red, orange	Much white space, but bright colors fill rest of picture: turquoise, blue, yellow, red, orange, brown, purple, green, black	Much orange, some brown, green, yellow, red, black	Extensive use of color: bright red, brown, orange, purple, blue, yellow, black, green
Use of White Space	White space is used to accent outline of characters and to provide irregular border	Boldly-colored characters stand out against vast, empty, white space	White space completely surrounds Simon and Pieperson/ machine	White space used only for clouds, Piewoman's bonnet, and definite border
Use of Line	Curved and straight lines combined to produce a sense of movement	Extensive use of vertical and horizontal lines; many lines are as straight as a ruler	Plenty of horizontal and vertical lines, some curved and round lines	Extensive use of curved and serpentine lines; straight, freehand lines form border and basket ropes
Use of Form and Shape	Full, round faces match the full, round pies; small, circular buttons	Use of right angles and round shapes and rectangles	Extensive use of rectangles; few circles	Plenty of oval-shaped forms; two long rectangles
Head Covering — Simon's	Pointed, felt cap with flimsy brim	Flat-topped hat	Tam-like cap	Pointed, striped, knitted cap, with top-knot
Head Covering — Pieman's	Chef's cap	Chef's cap	None	White, drawstring bonnet

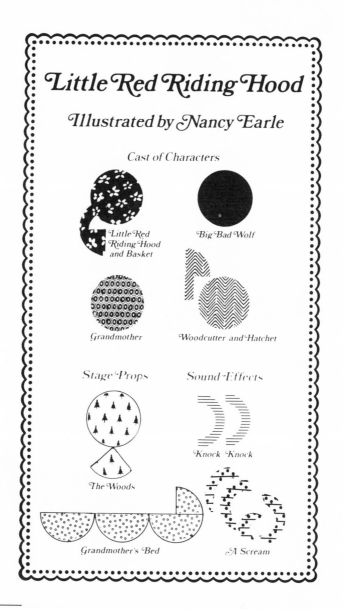

Reprinted with permission of the International Reading Association from *Journal of Reading*, November 1974, pp. 106-113.

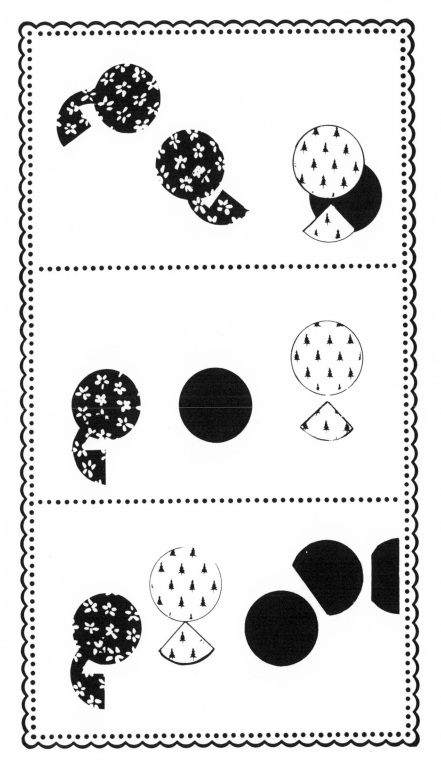

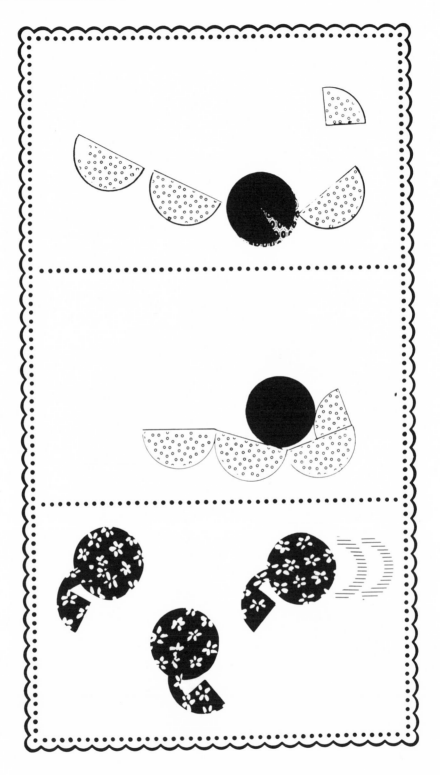

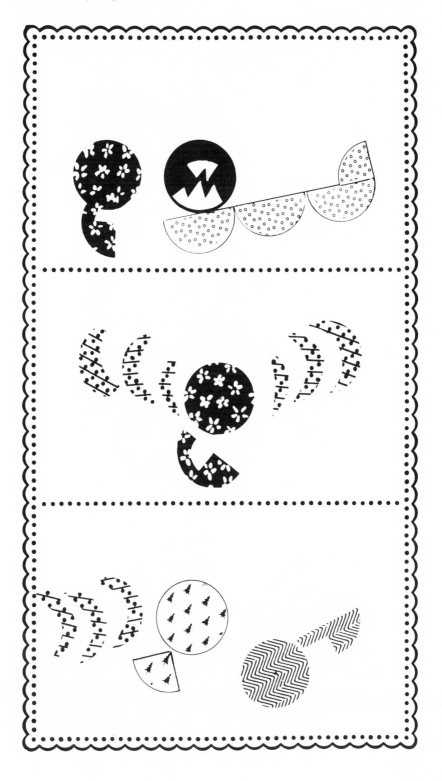

BIBLIOGRAPHY

Association for Educational Communications and Technology (AECT). 1126 16th Street, NW, Washington, DC 20036.

The Association has a variety of print and nonprint about visual literacy materials and programs. Write to the organization for an annotated listing of their publications.

The Audio-Visual Equipment Directory (198-). Fairfax, VA: National Audio-Visual Association (NAVA).

This annual publication is a listing and description of hardware available from members and nonmembers of NAVA, the trade organization of the AV industry. The directory is designed to help buyers make cost-effective decisions on the purchase and use of equipment. No implication is made that the directory includes all equipment available. Endorsement is not implied, nor does omission imply lack of approval.

Audiovisual Market Place: A Multimedia Guide. New York: Bowker, 1980.

A compendium of nonprint, *AVMP* is updated every year and includes complete information on audiovisual software and hardware. The reference section contains a calendar for nonprint events during the year, reference books and directories, periodicals and trade journals, national, regional, and state associations, funding sources, awards, festivals, and a glossary of terms.

"A-V Equipment Self-Instruction Packets." Eleven sound filmstrips. Random House Miller-Brody, 400 Hahn Road, Westminister, MD 21157. n.d.

These self-instructional packets are intended for use by students or teachers who wish to gain competency in equipment operation. Step-by-step instructions along with a diagram of the equipment make the units useful. Equipment covered includes the cassette recorder, record player, filmstrip viewer, super 8mm film loop projector, opaque projector, slide carousel projector, and reel-to-reel tape recorder.

Bell, Jo Ann. "Media Mix: Students Learn about Books from Tapes." *Top of the News* 27 (June 1971):388-94.

In this article, the author discusses the way a district goes about building a personal collection of book talks available on audiotape. She gives information on preparation and duplication of the tapes, reasons for preparing the tapes, and procedures for using the tapes in the media centers.

Brown, J. W., Lewis, R. B., and Harcleroad, F. F. *A V Instruction: Technology, Media, and Methods.* 5th ed. New York: McGraw-Hill, 1977.

This is a textbook that presents "an overview of media used in instruction and communication." It may also be used as a reference tool for teachers and librarians wishing to locate information on the role of media in various instructional programs, on selection, production, and use of individual media, or on future trends of media and telecommunication systems. Of particular value is the reference section, which covers such items as operating audiovisual equipment, duplicating processes, photographic equipment and techniques, physical facilities, classified directory of sources, and references.

Brown, James W., and Lewis, Richard B. *A V Instructional Manual for Independent Study.* 5th ed. New York: McGraw-Hill, 1977.

The manual may be used as a guide for creating instructional materials, for selection and use of ready-made materials, or for equipment operation. Also included are performance checklists for commonly-used equipment. Each unit in the manual is concise with specific references to the textbook, *A V Instruction*, for additional reading. Black-and-white illustrations and line drawings enhance the text.

"Creating Slide/Tape Programs." Sound filmstrip. Washington, DC: AECT, 1980.

The filmstrip with audiocassette describes the process of producing a slide/tape program. Ideas on scripting, photography, and audio production are covered.

"The Creative Eye." Three sound filmstrips. Society for Visual Education, 1345 Diversey Parkway, Chicago, IL 60614. n.d.

The series of filmstrips challenges students to see familiar places and things in new ways. Photographs encourage children to use their imaginations.

Cyr, Don. *Teaching Your Children Photography: A Step-by-Step Guide.* Garden City, NY: American Photographic Book, 1977.

This collection of 25 projects involving a variety of photographic and non-photographic techniques is perfect for the parent or teacher who knows very little or even nothing about the camera and photography but wants to learn and have fun at the same time. The projects are easy to follow and the text is well illustrated. The author has covered such projects as sun pictures, color slides without a camera, pinhole camera and pictures, information on the less-than-a-dollar camera and games that challenge the viewer to see everyday objects in new ways. A brief annotated sources and resources section is also included.

Dickson, Helen K. *Shopper's Flyer for Elementary School Career Education Curriculum Materials.* Watertown, SD: South Dakota Career Education Project, n.d. 11p. (ED 092 744; Reprint: EDRS).

Prepared for persons "shopping" for elementary school level career education materials, the guide has approximately 84 entries, including books, book and pamphlet series, kits, films, filmstrips, records, cassettes, songbooks, picture-story prints, games and toys, and other materials. Entries are listed by grade level where appropriate and under these headings: making things with tools, assistance in lesson design, assistance in occupational information, selecting media center and classroom reading, purchasing textbooks for all levels, and learning kits and audiovisual aids to teach self-awareness, career awareness, beginning competency, acceptance of self, career awareness in the city and community, appreciation and attitudes, and economic awareness. Title, publishing company, and price are indicated for each entry.

Dondis, D. A. *A Primer of Visual Literacy.* Cambridge, MA: MIT Press, 1973.
    This handbook is a basic guide to an understanding of the role visual literacy plays in the communication process and how it is displayed in the visual arts.

Eastman Kodak Company. Education Markets Services, Rochester, NY 14650.
    The Eastman Kodak Company is continuously revising and adding to their print and nonprint holdings for circulation and use by teachers and library media specialists. Costs for loan or purchase are typically inexpensive. Many items are free, such as *Montage: Imagination in Learning*, a newsletter for educators showing students using and producing their own nonprint; *Teaching Tips from Teachers!*, a compilation of ideas sent in by teachers of their methods of using photography in the classroom; and *Your Programs from Kodak*, a catalog of free-loan film and slide programs produced in a classroom situation and now distributed by Kodak for anyone in schools to view.

Fransecky, Roger B., and Debes, John L. *Visual Literacy: A Way to Learn—A Way to Teach.* Washington, DC: AECT, 1972.
    The authors introduce the reader to techniques for using visual literacy in the curriculum. Also included is a short discussion of some of the research done in this area as well as a list of references for further reading.

Gaffrey, Maureen, and Laybourne, Gerry Bond. *What to Do When the Lights Go On.* Phoenix, AZ: Oryx Press, 1980.
    The authors have created a recipe book for people who want to combine art activities and film with children. It gives film users practical, child-tested information about what children perceive in films and what activities can be used to follow a film screening.

Gassan, Arnold. *Handbook for Contemporary Photography.* 4th ed. Rochester, NY: Light Impressions, 1977.
    This handbook begins with such basics as loading the camera, darkroom development, printing, and enlargement and includes a discussion on storing prints and negatives. The major portion of the book, however, covers advanced controls and special processes for the more serious students of photography.

Getting It on Video/Series I & II. Media Systems, Inc., 3637 East 7800 South, Salt Lake City, UT 84121. n.d.
    Each series contains six sound filmstrips that explain how to use video equipment. Individual units contain such information as the video camera, recorder, portable and single camera systems, graphics for television, audio for television, planning a television production, set design, etc. For each filmstrip there is an instructional manual setting forth the objectives, teaching strategies, and tests and filmstrip scripts. This company also produces other visual aides helpful in specific equipment operation.

Guide Book: 1973 Edition. Bloomington, IN: National Instructional Television Center, 1973. 32p. (ED 070 276; Reprint: EDRS).
    The National Instructional Television Center (NIT) aims to reduce the time of bringing about educational innovation from the usual 15 years, achieved through traditional means like pre-service education and workshops, to 5 years.

Its procedure in doing this is to identify significant ideas and translate them into useful television programs. This booklet describes NIT courses, which consist of television series. The course descriptions are organized by subject matter. For each, the appropriate audience level (which ranges from primary through senior high school as well as teacher training and higher education) is indicated. Also included are an index of courses by grade level and subject matter, a list of NIT prices, procedures, and policies, and descriptions of NIT services and professional publicatons and films, which deal with instructional television.

Harwood, Don. *Everything You Always Wanted to Know about Video Tape Recording.* 2nd ed. New York: VTR Publishing, 1975.

The book is a technical guide to the use of video tape recorders (vtr) without using technical language. The author explains the vtr's uses, includes charts and instructions for using the separate pieces of equipment, production and editing techniques, and a chapter on preventative maintenance.

Hobson, Andrew, and Hobson, Mark. *Film Animation as a Hobby.* New York: Sterling Publishing, 1975.

The Hobson brothers have written a book that covers all the areas of making animated films. Basic animation techniques, sample clips, and equipment are discussed. The book is especially appropriate for individuals with little to no experience in making animated movies.

Kemp, Jerrold E. *Planning and Producing Audiovisual Materials.* 4th ed. New York: Harper & Row, 1980.

This work proposes to "provide information and experiences that will enable the reader to gain competencies" regarding purposes of using audiovisual materials, reasons for producing them, and planning for their use and production including reasons for the use of a particular medium and instructions for fundamental skills and their application. Each chapter is organized to describe and/or explain a specific area of study. Most are well illustrated with graphic displays of the techniques and intended results.

Langford, Michael. *Visual Aids and Photography in Education; A Visual Aids Manual for Teachers and Learners.* New York: Hastings House, 1973.

The author's twofold purpose for the book is "to show in detail how today's equipment can be used by teachers themselves to make aids, and by learners to expand their knowledge and develop individual creative abilities." Although much of the equipment discussed is somewhat outdated and prices are given as of 1973 (in pounds), the detailed step-by-step methods for making all types of visual aids would be useful for anyone beginning to explore production.

Laybourne, Kit, and Cianciolo, Pauline, eds. *Doing the Media: A Portfolio of Activities, Ideas and Resources.* New rev. ed. New York: McGraw-Hill, 1979.

The editors maintain that *Doing the Media* is "intended to serve as both a practical text in media education courses and as a portfolio of ideas for the professional teacher, media specialist, librarian, and others engaged in formal or informal educational activities." The 18 contributors show how nonprint may be integrated into both the elementary and secondary curriculum to make students aware of the influence mass media has over their daily lives. The book provides excellent details and step-by-step procedures for *doing* photography, film, video, sound, and other media. The seventh section deals with the process of designing

"an integrated media arts curriculum." The final section of the book is an annotated resources listing of print and nonprint materials, periodicals, organizations,
and media distributors.

Linton, Dolores, and Linton, David. *Practical Guide to Classroom Media.* Dayton, OH: Pflaum/Standard, 1971.

The authors have divided the book into two logical divisions: "Laying the
Groundwork for Media Involvement" and "Involving Media in the Classroom."
Although the illustrations included add very little to the meaning of the text, the
value of the book rests in the variety of student activities and projects discussed.

McLaughlin, Frank, ed. *The Mediate Teacher: Seminal Essays on Creative
Teaching.* Philadelphia, PA: North American, 1975.

The editor has compiled a collection of essays "about being a special kind of
teacher—one who is or intends to be far more attuned and attentive than the
average faculty member." A wide variety of topics are presented from "a model
for multi-media learning" to "a primer on games" to "films for consciousness raising." The main thrust of the work appears to be for teachers "who recognize that
they must be constantly learning and growing if they expect to effectively touch
the lives of their students." The book is an essential survival tool for any teacher.

McLuhan, Marshall. *Understanding Media: The Extensions of Man.* New York:
McGraw-Hill, 1964.

Although the original publication is now over 16 years old, this book is basic
to any secondary collection for students wishing to explore the impact of nonprint on society. The author sets forth his own philosophy and then shows how
this opinion is mirrored in the media. McLuhan is widely quoted, and the work
itself should continue to be a center for controversy and discussion for years to
come.

Miller, Hannah. *Films in the Classroom: A Practical Guide.* Metuchen, NJ:
Scarecrow, 1979.

In addition to the coverage given to film in this guide, the author has also included a beginning chapter on nonprint media equipment that covers such information as standards and maintenance of hardware and criteria for judging software selection. There are also six appendices that list details such as organizations
helping teachers, students, and librarians understand the use of film, professional
journals, free and inexpensive sources of films and distributors. The major portion of the text discusses such topics as "film techniques," "types of film," choosing, securing, showing, using, and making films for the classroom.

Media Review Digest. Ann Arbor, MI: Pierian Press, 1973- .

MRD is a basic indexing tool to locate reviews of nonprint appearing in over
200 periodicals. Divisions in the index are according to format: films and
videotapes, filmstrips, records and tapes, and miscellaneous media. Bibliographic
information is given for each entry.

"Media Review." 343 Manville Road, Pleasantville, NY 10570.

This reviewing tool is intended to aid librarians in making nonprint pur-
chases. Monthly supplements offer program summaries and evaluations, new
ideas, current funding information, and reviews of professional books.

Minor, Ed, and Frye, Harvey R. *Techniques for Producing Visual Instructional Media*. 2nd ed. New York: McGraw-Hill, 1977.

The book is a step-by-step approach both for the person without graphic skills and the professional seeking new ways to solve problems of visual media production. The directions for each process are described concisely and clearly with accompanying line drawings. There are an extensive glossary of terminology, a bibliography and mediagraphy covering the production area, as well as an address directory of distributors ánd suppliers of materials.

Minor, Edward. *Handbook for Preparing Visual Media*. 2nd ed. New York: McGraw-Hill, 1978.

The author discusses techniques for illustrating, mounting and laminating materials, lettering and printing, coloring, and producing transparencies for projection and display. Each technique is explained in elaborate detail with specific line drawings accompanying the text for reinforcement.

Morrow, James, and Suid, Murray. *Media & Kids: Real-World Learning in Schools*. Rochelle Park, NJ: Hayden, 1977.

The authors maintain in their preface that the aim of this book is "to bridge the gap between creativity and the curriculum." The introductory essay to the volume titled "Why the medium is not the message" by Morrow sets forth his "vision of the classroom as a place where active production in all media is regarded as a natural way to learn." Two introductory chapters develop a model for multimedia learning and a consideration of pedagogical questions that might influence integration of media production in the classroom. Individual chapters are devoted to design, print, photography, radio, movies, television, and media and people.

National Center for Audio Tapes. University of Colorado, Stadium Building, Boulder, CO 80302. [Most current catalog].

The catalog is a compilation of audiotapes for duplication and sale by the National Center for Audio Tapes. The collection is arranged by subject areas with an individual entry description for each tape: title, stock number, producer, broadcast restrictions, grade level, description of contents, and running time. Titles may be ordered either on cassette or reels. Prices include duplication, tape, box with label, mailer, and postage.

National Information Center for Educational Media (NICEM). University of Southern California, University Park, Los Angeles, CA 90007.

NICEM provides indexes to all types of educational media: 16mm films, filmstrips, overhead transparencies, audiotapes, videotapes, records, motion picture cartridges, and slides. The publications are available and frequently updated in hard copy or microfiche. The file is also accessible through the Dialog database information retrieval service for $70.00 per online connect hour.

Oates, S. C. *Audiovisual Equipment Self-Instruction Manual*. 4th ed. Dubuque, IA: W. C. Brown, 1979.

This is one of the most up-to-date compilations of specific models of equipment by type on the market. The manual may be used for self-instruction or for reference when a problem develops during actual operation. Each unit is followed by a quiz to test the user's understanding of the printed text. Single black-and-white illustrations make the instructions easy to follow.

Phillipson, Willard D., and Teach, Beverly, eds. *Educational Film Locator of the Consortium of University Film Centers and R. R. Bowker Company.* 2nd ed. New York: Bowker, 1980.

The tool is "a union list of the titles held by member libraries of the Consortium ... , and a compilation and standardization of their separate catalogs, representing film holdings with their geographic locations." The compilation contains a detailed user's guide that explains the three main approaches to locating information: subject, title and series, and other special features. It should serve as a valuable reference tool for the media specialist who 1) must locate rental sources for 16mm films; 2) is called upon to formulate subject mediagraphies of 16mm titles appropriate for a particular audience; 3) desires to supply the viewer with a descriptive annotation before ordering; 4) needs to verify bibliographic information for cataloging; 5) seeks to identify films that have been produced as a series; or 6) wishes to locate foreign film titles.

Rice, Susan, and Mukerji, Rose, eds. *Children Are Centers for Understanding Media.* Washington, DC: Association for Childhood Education International, 1973.

This compilation documents the ongoing growth and development of the Center for Understanding Media, which "attempts through its activities to close the gap between the world of school and the world of the new information media." Many of the articles written for this publication were also included in *Doing the Media.* The articles cover a broad spectrum of media production by children of all ages from filmmaking to unusual audiotapes to tap the imagination of the young producers. A unique inclusion is a chapter on flipbooks as a first step to animation. The "Resources for Further Study" is an annotated listing of media, 12 of which have been starred for a "Basic Media Library."

Roach, Helen. *Spoken Records.* 3rd ed. Metuchen, NJ: Scarecrow, 1970.

Although the compilation is ten years old, this is the best tool for selection and evaluation of spoken records across a variety of subject areas. Teachers and media specialists would find this tool useful for establishing a basic spoken record library and for reference to recordings of lectures, speeches, interviews, and authors reading their own works. The author also has a comprehensive analysis of classical and modern literature and plays appropriate for use with preschool through senior high school.

Rosenberg, K. D., and Doskey, J. S. *Media Equipment: A Guide and Dictionary.* Littleton, CO: Libraries Unlimited, 1976.

The book is divided into three major sections: general criteria for equipment selection; specific criteria for individual types of equipment; and a dictionary of terms related to media equipment. The sample checklist forms for individual pieces of equipment would be especially useful when the teacher or media specialist is considering a new purchase.

Rufsvold, Margaret I. *Guides to Educational Media: Films, Filmstrips, Kinescopes, Phonodiscs, Phonotapes, Programmed Instruction Materials, Slides, Transparencies and Videotapes.* 4th ed. Chicago, IL: ALA, 1977.

The purpose of this book as stated by its compiler is "to identify and describe catalogs, indexes, lists, and reviewing services which systematically provide information about educational media." Bibliographies and catalogs included in the guide review all of the formats included in the title. The entries are listed in an author, subject, and title index.

Schillaci, Anthony, and Culkin, John M., eds. *Films Deliver: Teaching Creatively with Film.* New York: Citation Press, 1970.

This compilation of articles is designed "to show interested teachers how to teach creatively through the use of the two most compelling media arts — film and television." The work is divided into three sections; the first is an overview of "What Films Can Do for Teachers and Students" in the curriculum. The other two sections discuss specific areas of the curriculum where films have been used, how to go about selecting appropriate titles, and actual student production activities. Appendices include a filmography of feature and short films, a bibliography of film study, and sample teachers' guides.

Schrank, Jeffrey, ed. *The Seed Catalog; A Guide to Teaching/Learning Materials.* Boston, MA: Beacon, 1974.

The editor, in his introduction to the catalog, proclaims that it is intended "for those in any situation who believe that learning takes place through involvement with a great variety of viewpoints and opinions." Learning, according to the editor, can take place by using both print and nonprint. The contents direct the reader to seek information on publications that "challenge, provoke, and entertain," organizations and little-known and unusual periodicals, audiotapes and the alternative radio movement, film, video, games, multimedia, and devices, such as posters, computers, and emotionmeters. The prices of the materials are "comparatively inexpensive rather than a $300 learning package."

Sive, Mary Robinson. *Selecting Instructional Media: A Guide to Audiovisual and Other Instructional Media Lists.* Littleton, CO: Libraries Unlimited, 1978.

The compiler has included 428 published lists of audiovisual and other instructional media appropriate for use with grades K through 12. Each entry contains a complete annotation stating the purpose, grade level, arrangement, subjects, entries, indexes, period covered, revision and updating, media represented, features, and subject terms. The book is intended to aid educators in the selection and purchase of media for curriculum development, for classroom instruction, and for building a collection.

Spirt, D. L. *Library/Media Manual.* New York: H. W. Wilson, 1979.

As the author points out in her introduction, the manual, "which provides instruction on how to get information from a wide variety of communication media, is for students ... who have had little or no instruction in the use of books and nonprint materials." The book is divided into chapters and subdivided into appropriate units with a quiz following each chapter to test for recall. The first chapter is especially helpful, titled "The Library Media Center." In it the author relates "policies, resources and organization" of a media center and "starting the research: using print and nonprint materials." Terminology to be used throughout the text is clearly defined. Chapter two deals with guides to use in accessing print and nonprint. Chapter three is devoted to specific reference books, and chapter four explains the research process: search strategy, taking notes, and formulating a mediagraphy.

Spitzing, Günter, and Steinorth, Karl. *Peter and His Camera.* Dobbs Ferry, NY: Morgan & Morgan, 1973.

This is a picture storybook centered around a young boy learning about his camera. The main character appears to be 10-12 years old, and the text is appropriate for this age range. The illustrations add clarity to the text and make the book visually appealing for its audience. Two closing sections, which the reader will find helpful, are included: "What Peter does to take good pictures" and "Terms used by camera fans."

"Tell Me What You See." Sound filmstrip. Washington, DC: AECT, 1975.

The program shows how visual literacy is used as a major part of the curriculum in the Milford, Ohio schools. (An article included in this compilation, "Seeing Sequentially: A Curriculum" by Roy Ferguson, also speaks to this experience.) Students learn about visual communications and how to use media to create their own unique message.

Thomas, James L., and Loring, Ruth M., eds. *Motivating Children and Young Adults to Read.* Phoenix, AZ: Oryx Press, 1979.

The book is a compilation of journal articles for teachers faced with the challenge of motivating youngsters to read. One section is devoted to the use of nonprint to entice the nonreader to read.

Thomas, James L. *Nonprint for Students, Teachers and Media Specialists: A Step-by-Step Approach.* Littleton, CO: Libraries Unlimited, 1982.

The author gives specific steps of the procedures for the production of nonprint projects useful in involving students and educators in the learning process. The following chapters are included: transparency lifts and story lamination; slide-tape presentations; filmstrip presentations; super 8mm movie productions; single-camera television programs; and dioramas. Detailed information is given on storyboarding, the materials and hardware needed for each project, and the potential costs.

To Help Them Learn. 16mm film. 21 mins. Color. Washington, DC: AECT & Association of Media Producers, 1977.

The movie shows, through discussion and demonstration, the rationale for using all formats of media to reach the individual student in the learning process. The film is fast-paced and shows teachers interacting with a variety of age groups.

Tyler-John, Martha. *Using Media in the Elementary Classroom.* Pullman, WA: Information Futures, 1979.

The author shows, through a series of mini-case studies, the ways in which elementary school teachers have successfully integrated all types of media into the curriculum "to maximize the child's learning opportunities."

The Video Source Book. Syosset, NY: National Video Clearinghouse, 1979.

Over 15,000 individual pre-recorded video program titles available on videotape or videodisc are included. The compilation is taken from distributors' catalogs and is therefore not a selection tool but a resource guide for locating useful titles in these formats. Titles are listed alphabetically with each carrying full bibliographic data and location information. A category index is supplied and divided into broad subject areas. A distributor index is also provided for ordering.

Wagner, Betty, and Stunard, Arthur. *Making and Using Inexpensive Classroom Media.* Palo Alto, CA: Education Today, 1976.

The authors contend that the book is for beginners who want to use a wide range of media. Their aim is "to help you feel comfortable enough with easy communication-oriented processes to show your students how to use them." The handbook has easy-to-follow instructions for making displays, multimedia shows, photography, movie making, and more. Simple line drawings and black-and-white illustrations of students working on the projects aid the user in understanding the concepts presented.

Wein, Jan, and Wein, Jeff. *The Big Picture: Photography and Slides in the Classroom.* Waitsfield, VT: Vermont Crossroads Press, 1977.

The authors explore the visual literacy process of young children gaining meaning from photography and slide preparation. Each section shows primary age children engaged in some aspect of the process being discussed.

"The Whys and Hows of Student Film Making." Two sound filmstrips. Random House Miller-Brody, 400 Hahn Road, Westminster, MD 21157. 1970.

This program is intended for use by teachers who wish to gain insight into the movie making process as it relates to classroom education and development of visual literacy skills. A paperback book on the basic techniques of filmmaking is also included.

Williams, Frank E. *Media Resource Book: The Total Creativity Program for Individualizing and Humanizing the Learning Process.* Volume 4. Englewood Cliffs, NJ: Educational Technology Publications, 1972. 77p. (ED 070 244 or available from: Educational Technology Publications, 140 Sylvan Ave., Englewood Cliffs, NJ 07632).

Books and films that are directly useful in producing the eight thinking-feeling processes of the cognitive-affective interaction (CAI) model on which this complete program is based are listed. (See ED 010 276 for the rationale for and discussion of this model.) Ninety-two books appropriate to the pupil processes and teaching strategies of the CAI model are listed along with suggested grade level and a short annotation. Seventy films are alphabetized by title. The films are also classified by pupil process and teaching strategy. Eighteen curriculum programs or materials designed to develop certain thinking-feeling processes are listed alphabetically by title of program or material.

Wiman, Raymond. *Instructional Materials; An Illustrated Handbook of Ideas, Skills, and Techniques for Producing and Using Audiovisual Materials.* Worthington, OH: C. A. Jones, 1972.

A how-to-do-it information manual for teachers and media specialists about photography, transparency production, lettering, drawing, bulletin boards, dry mounting, and operation of equipment. Simple line drawings make the handbook practical and easy to follow.

Wittich, W. A., and Schuller, C. F. *Instructional Technology: Its Nature and Use.* 5th ed. New York: Harper & Row, 1973.

The textbook is intended as a bridge between theory and practice in showing how media and technology might be used "in actual teaching involving a variety of instructional strategies." The authors show how instructional technology is used to improve learning and how essential the teacher is to the effective use of this technology. The majority of the work deals with individual media as they relate to the learning process. *A Student Production Guide* has been developed to reinforce the main text.

APPENDIX I:
A SELECTIVE LISTING OF
PERIODICALS EVALUATING NONPRINT

The following periodicals useful for the school curriculum include a wide variety of media—both print and nonprint. In order to see if a specific title meets a need in the selection of nonprint, the reader is encouraged to write to the individual publisher for a sample copy and price schedule.

AMP REPORTS	Association of Media Producers, Inc. Suite 515 1707 L Street, NW Washington, DC 20036
AV GUIDE	Educational Screen, Inc. 434 S. Wabash Avenue Chicago, IL 60605
AMERICAN BIOLOGY TEACHER	National Association of Biology Teachers 11250 Roger Bacon Drive Reston, VA 22090
AMERICAN CINEMATOGRAPHER	American Society of Cinematographers 1782 N. Orange Drive Hollywood, CA 90028
AMERICAN FILM	American Film Institute John F. Kennedy Center for the Performing Arts Washington, DC 20566
AMERICAN RECORD GUIDE	ARG Publishing, Inc. One Windsor Place Melville, NY 11746
THE ANIMATOR	Northwest Film Study Center Northland Art Museum Southwest Park & Madison Portland, OR 97205
ARTS & ACTIVITIES	Publishers' Development Corporation Camino de la Reina, Suite 200 San Diego, CA 92108
ATHLETIC JOURNAL	Athletic Journal Publishing Company 1719 Howard Street Evanston, IL 60202

AUDIO   North American Publishing Company
                                        401 N. Broad Street
                                        Philadelphia, PA 19108

AUDIO-VISUAL COMMUNICATIONS   United Business Publications, Inc.
                                        475 Park Avenue South
                                        New York, NY 10016

AUDIO-VISUAL JOURNAL   Audio-Visual Library Service
                                        University of Minnesota
                                        3300 University Avenue, SE
                                        Minneapolis, MN 55414

AUDIO VISUAL NEWS BRIEFS   Association of National Advertisers
                                        155 E. 44th Street
                                        New York, NY 10017

BETTER RADIO & TELEVISION   National Association for Better
                                          Broadcasting
                                        Box 43640
                                        Los Angeles, CA 90043

BOOKLIST   American Library Association
                                        50 E. Huron Street
                                        Chicago, IL 60611

CATHOLIC FILM NEWSLETTER   Office for Film & Broadcasting
                                        U.S. Catholic Conference
                                        1011 First Avenue, Suite 1300
                                        New York, NY 10022

THE CLEARINGHOUSE   Helen Dwight Reid Educational
                                          Foundation
                                        4000 Albermarle Street, NW
                                        Washington, DC 20016

CURRENT INDEX TO JOURNALS   Oryx Press
  IN EDUCATION   2214 North Central at Encanto
                                        Phoenix, AZ 85004

CURRICULUM PRODUCT REVIEW   McGraw-Hill, Inc.
                                        230 W. Monroe Street
                                        Suite 1100
                                        Chicago, IL 60606

EDUCATIONAL & INDUSTRIAL   C. S. Tepfer Publishing Company, Inc.
  TELEVISION   51 Sugar Hollow Road
                                        Danbury, CT 06810

EDUCATIONAL DIGEST   Maclean Hunter Ltd.
                                        481 University Avenue
                                        Toronto, Ontario M5W 1A7, Canada

EDUCATIONAL SCREEN &   Educational Screen, Inc.
AUDIOVISUAL GUIDE   434 S. Wabash Avenue
                                        Chicago, IL 60605

EDUCATIONAL TECHNOLOGY   Educational Technology Publications, Inc.
                                        140 Sylvan Avenue
                                        Englewood Cliffs, NJ 07632

EFLA EVALUATIONS	Educational Film Library Association, Inc. 43 W. 61st Street New York, NY 10023
ELEMENTARY ENGLISH	National Council of Teachers of English 1111 Kenyon Road Urbana, IL 61801
ELEMENTARY SCHOOL JOURNAL	University of Chicago Press 5835 Kimbark Avenue Chicago, IL 60637
ENGLISH JOURNAL	National Council of Teachers of English 1111 Kenyon Road Urbana, IL 61801
EPIEgram: MATERIALS	The Educational Products Information Exchange (EPIE) Institute 475 Riverside Drive New York, NY 10027
ETV NEWSLETTER	C. S. Tepfer Publishing Company, Inc. 607 Main Street Ridgefield, CT 06877
EXCEPTIONAL CHILDREN	The Council for Exceptional Children 1920 Association Drive Reston, VA 22091
FILM COMMENT	The Film Society of Lincoln Center 1865 Broadway New York, NY 10023
FILM LIBRARY QUARTERLY	Film Library Information Council Box 348 Radio City Station New York, NY 10019
FILM NEWS	Film News Company 250 W. 57th Street, Suite 2202 New York, NY 10019
FILM QUARTERLY	University of California Press Berkeley, CA 94720
G P NEWSLETTER	Great Plains National Instructional Television Library Box 80669 Lincoln, NE 68501
GRADE TEACHER	Macmillan Professional Magazines, Inc. 1 Fawcett Place Greenwich, CT 06830
HIGH FIDELITY MAGAZINE	ABC Leisure Magazine, Inc. The Publishing House Great Barrington, MA 01230
HORN BOOK MAGAZINE	Horn Book, Inc. Park Square Building 31st Street & James Avenue Boston, MA 02116

INDUSTRIAL EDUCATION

Macmillan Professional Magazines, Inc.
1 Fawcett Place
Greenwich, CT 06830

INSTRUCTIONAL INNOVATOR

Association for Educational
    Communications and Technology
1126 16th Street, NW
Washington, DC 20036

INSTRUCTOR

The Instructor Publications, Inc.
Seven Bank Street
Dansville, NY 14437

INTERNATIONAL JOURNAL OF
INSTRUCTIONAL MEDIA

Baywood Publishing Company
120 Marine Street
Farmingdale, NY 11735

JOURNAL OF EDUCATIONAL
TECHNOLOGY SYSTEMS

Baywood Publishing Company
120 Marine Street
Farmingdale, NY 11735

JOURNAL OF HEALTH, PHYSICAL
EDUCATION, RECREATION

American Association for Health,
    Physical Education, and Recreation
1201 16th Street, NW
Washington, DC 20036

JOURNAL OF GEOGRAPHY

National Council for Geographic
    Education
Department of Geography
Western Illinois University
Macomb, IL 61455

JOURNAL OF LEARNING
DISABILITIES

Professional Press, Inc.
101 E. Ontario Street
Chicago, IL 60611

JOURNAL OF POPULAR FILM
& TELEVISION

Center for Popular Culture
Bowling Green State University
Bowling Green, OH 43403

K-eight

134 North 13th Street
Philadelphia, PA 19107

K-3 BULLETIN OF TEACHING IDEAS
& MATERIALS

Parker Publishing Company
Prentice-Hall
West Nyack, NY 10994

LANDERS FILM REVIEWS

Landers Associates
Box 69760
Los Angeles, CA 90069

LANGUAGE ARTS

National Council of Teachers of English
1111 Kenyon Road
Urbana, IL 61801

LEARNING

Education Today Company, Inc.
530 University Avenue
Palo Alto, CA 94301

LIBRARY TECHNOLOGY REPORTS

American Library Association
50 E. Huron Street
Chicago, Il 60611

LISTENING POST	Bro-Dart, Inc. 1236 S. Hatcher City of Industry, CA 91748
LJ/SLJ HOTLINE	R. R. Bowker Company 1180 Avenue of the Americas New York, NY 10036
MAN/SOCIETY/TECHNOLOGY: A JOURNAL OF INDUSTRIAL EDUCATION	American Industrial Arts Association, Inc. 1201 16th Street, NW Washington, DC 20036
MATHEMATICS TEACHER	National Council of Teachers of Mathematics 1906 Association Drive Reston, VA 22091
MEDIA & METHODS	North American Publishing Company 401 Broad Street Philadelphia, PA 19108
MEDIA DIGEST	National Film & Video Center 4321 Sykesville Road Finksburg, MD 21048
MEDIA MIX	Claretian Publications 221 W. Madison Chicago, IL 60606
MODERN LANGUAGE JOURNAL	National Federation of Modern Language Teachers Associations 30A McKenna Building University of Colorado Boulder, CO 80309
NOTES	Music Library Association, Inc. 343 S. Main Street, Room 205 Ann Arbor, MI 48108
PREVIEWS	R. R. Bowker Company 1180 Avenue of the Americas New York, NY 10036
PTST	Prime Time School Television 120 South LaSalle Street Chicago, IL 60603
PUBLIC TELECOMMUNICATIONS REVIEW	National Association of Educational Broadcasters 1346 Connecticut Avenue, NW Washington, DC 20036
RADICAL SOFTWARE/CHANGING CHANNELS	Gordon & Breach Science Publishers Ltd. 42 William IV Street London WC2, England
RECORDED VISUAL INSTRUCTION	Great Plains National Instructional Television Library (GPN) Box 80669 Lincoln, NE 68501

RELIGION TEACHER'S JOURNAL

Twenty Third Publications
Box 180
West Mystic, CT 06388

RESOURCES IN EDUCATION

Educational Resources Information Center
National Institute of Education
Washington, DC 20208

ROCKINGCHAIR

Cupola Productions
Box 27-K
Philadelphia, PA 19105

SCHOOL ARTS MAGAZINE

Davis Publishing, Inc.
Printers Building
50 Portland Street
Worcester, MA 01608

SCHOOL LIBRARY JOURNAL

R. R. Bowker Company
1180 Avenue of the Americas
New York, NY 10036

SCHOOL MEDIA QUARTERLY

American Library Association
50 E. Huron Street
Chicago, IL 60611

SCHOOL PRODUCT NEWS

Industrial Publishing Company
614 Superior W.
Cleveland, OH 44113

SCIENCE ACTIVITIES

HELDREF Publications
4000 Albemarle Street, NW, Suite 510
Washington, DC 20016

SCIENCE BOOKS & FILMS

American Association for the
   Advancement of Science
1776 Massachusetts Avenue, NW
Washington, DC 20036

SCIENCE TEACHER

National Science Teachers Association
1742 Connecticut Avenue, NW
Washington, DC 20009

SIGHTLINES

Educational Film Library Association
43 W. 61st Street
New York, NY 10023

SNEAK PREVIEW, THE MEDIA
   DIGEST

National Educational Film Center
Finksburg, MD 21048

SOCIAL EDUCATION

National Council for the Social Studies
1515 Wilson Boulevard
Arlington, VA 22209

SOCIAL STUDIES

McKinley Publishing Company
112 S. New Broadway
Brooklawn, NJ 08030

STEREO REVIEW

Ziff-Davis Publishing Company
One Park Avenue
New York, NY 10016

SUPER-8 FILMMAKER

PMS Publishing Company, Inc.
3161 Fillmore Street
San Francisco, CA 94123

TEACHER MAGAZINE

Macmillan Professional Magazines, Inc.
77 Bedford Street
Stamford, CT 06901

TEACHING EXCEPTIONAL
  CHILDREN

Council for Exceptional Children
1920 Association Drive
Reston, VA 22091

TODAY'S CATHOLIC TEACHER

Peter Li, Inc.
2451 E. River Road
Dayton, OH 45439

TODAY'S EDUCATION

Journal of the National Education
  Association
1201 16th Street, NW
Washington, DC 20036

TOP OF THE NEWS

American Library Association
50 E. Huron Street
Chicago, IL 60611

TRAINING FILM PROFILES

Olympic Media Information
71 W. 23rd Street
New York, NY 10010

TV GUIDE

TV Guide
Box 400
Radnor, PA 19088

VIDEO NEWS

Phillips Publishing, Inc.
8401 Connecticut Avenue, Suite 707
Washington, DC 20015

APPENDIX II:
ORGANIZATIONS CONCERNED
WITH NONPRINT

Name & Address	Publication(s)
Academy for Educational Development, Inc. 680 Fifth Avenue New York, NY 10019	
Action for Children's Television (ACT) 46 Austin Street Newtonville, MA 02160	NEWSLETTER
Agency for Instructional Television Box A Bloomington, IN 47401	AIT NEWSLETTER
American Association of Museums 1055 Thomas Jefferson Street, NW Washington, DC 20007	MUSEUM NEWS
American Association of School Administrators 1801 N. Moore Street Arlington, VA 22209	THE SCHOOL ADMINISTRATOR
American Association of School Librarians (AASL) 50 E. Huron Street Chicago, IL 60611	SCHOOL MEDIA QUARTERLY
The American Film Institute The John F. Kennedy Center for the Performing Arts Washington, DC 20566	AMERICAN FILM
American Foundation for the Blind, Inc. 15 W. 16th Street New York, NY 10011	AFB NEWSLETTER; JOURNAL OF VISUAL IMPAIRMENT & BLINDNESS; WASHINGTON REPORT
American Library Association (ALA) 50 E. Huron Street Chicago, IL 60611	AMERICAN LIBRARIES; BOOKLIST; TOP OF THE NEWS
American Science Film Association 3624 Market Street Philadelphia, PA 19104	ASFA NOTES

American Theatre Association 1000 Vermont Avenue, NW Washington, DC 20005	SECONDARY SCHOOL THEATRE JOURNAL; CHILDREN'S THEATRE REVIEW
Association for Childhood Education International 3615 Wisconsin Avenue, NW Washington, DC 20016	CHILDHOOD EDUCATION
Association for Educational Communications and Technology (AECT) 1126 16th Street, NW Washington, DC 20036	INSTRUCTIONAL INNOVATOR
Association for Supervision and Curriculum Development 1701 K Street, NW, Suite 1100 Washington, DC 20006	EDUCATIONAL LEADERSHIP
Association of Media Producers 1707 L Street, NW, Suite 515 Washington, DC 20006	AMP REPORTS
Broadcasting Foundation of America 52 Vanderbilt Avenue, Suite 1810 New York, NY 10017	
Carnegie Council on Children 1619 Broadway New York, NY 10019	
Catholic Library Association 461 W. Lancaster Avenue Haverford, PA 19041	CATHOLIC LIBRARY WORLD
Center for Understanding Media 66 Fifth Avenue New York, NY 10014	
Children's Television Workshop (CTW) One Lincoln Plaza New York, NY 10023	
Consortium of University Film Centers c/o Visual Aids Service University of Illinois Champaign, IL 61820	EDUCATIONAL FILM LOCATOR
Educational Film Library Association, Inc. 43 W. 61st Street New York, NY 10023	SIGHTLINES
Educational Resources Information Center (ERIC) National Institute of Education Washington, DC 20208	RESOURCES IN EDUCATION; CURRENT INDEX TO JOURNALS IN EDUCATION; THESAURUS OF ERIC DESCRIPTORS; RESOURCES IN INFORMATION EDUCATION

Educational Products Information
  Exchange Institute (EPIE)
475 Riverside Drive
New York, NY 10027

EPIEgram; EQUIPMENT

Film Library Information Council
Box 348
Radio City Station
New York, NY 10019

FILM LIBRARY QUARTERLY

Foundation to Improve Television
50 Congress Street
Boston, MA 02109

Foxfire Fund
Route 1
Rabun Gap, GA 30568

FOXFIRE

Industrial Audio-Visual Association
Box 656
Downtown Station
Chicago, IL 60690

International Quorum of Motion Picture
  Producers (IQ)
Box 395
Oakton, VA 22124

QUORUM QUOTES

International Tape Exchange
834 Ruddiman Avenue
North Muskegon, MI 49445

PUPILS SPEAK TO PUPILS AROUND
THE WORLD

Media Action Research Center (MARC)
475 Riverside Drive, Suite 1370
New York, NY 10027

Media Center for Children
43 W. 61st Street
New York, NY 10023

YOUNG VIEWERS

The Modern Language Association of
  America
62 Fifth Avenue
New York, NY 10011

PMLA; MLA NEWSLETTER

Music Educators National Conference
1902 Association Drive
Reston, VA 22091

MUSIC EDUCATORS JOURNAL

National Association of Elementary
  School Principals
1801 N. Moore Street
Arlington, VA 22209

THE NATIONAL ELEMENTARY
PRINCIPAL

National Audio-Visual Association
  (NAVA)
3150 Spring Street
Fairfax, VA 22031

AUDIO-VISUAL EQUIPMENT
DIRECTORY; A-V CONNECTION;
THE GUIDE TO FEDERAL FUNDS
FOR AUDIO-VISUAL PROGRAMS

National Council of Teachers of English
1111 Kenyon Road
Urbana, IL 61801

LANGUAGE ARTS; ENGLISH
JOURNAL

National Film Board of Canada
Box 6100
Montreal, Quebec H3C 3H5, Canada

National Public Radio
2025 M Street, NW
Washington, DC 20036

Prime Time School Television (PTST)
120 S. LaSalle Street
Chicago, IL 60603

Society for Applied Learning Technology
50 Culpeper Street
Warrenton, VA 22186

JOURNAL OF EDUCATIONAL
TECHNOLOGY SYSTEMS

Workshop for Learning Things
5 Bridge Street
Watertown, MA 02172

CATALOG

Youth Film Distribution Center
43 W. 16th Street
New York, NY 10011

CATALOG

APPENDIX III:
PRODUCERS OF NONPRINT MATERIALS

Most of the producers included in this listing supply a wide variety of media. Those usually limited to one medium can be easily located by their descriptive titles; for example, "color slides" or "films." Also, the subject areas indicated are those appropriate for this compilation and audience. Some of the producers do provide materials in other areas and for undergraduate and professional programs.

Grade range abbreviations used in the listing:

Pr - Preschool

K - Kindergarten

P - Primary

I   - Intermediate

Name & Address	Grade Range	the arts	education	humanities	language arts/reading	library science/media	mathematics	music	physical education/sports	science	social sciences
ABC Media Concepts 1330 Avenue of the Americas New York, NY 10019	P-I	x	x	x	x				x	x	x
ABT Publications 55 Wheeler Street Cambridge, MA 02138	P-I		x			x	x				x
Academy Films Inc Box 38753 Hollywood, CA 90038	Pr-I	x		x	x					x	x
Acorn Films Inc 33 Union Square W. New York, NY 10003	I								x	x	
Advance Process Supply Company 400 N. Noble Street Chicago, IL 60622	P-I	x									
Aero Products Research Inc 11201 Hindry Avenue Los Angeles, CA 90045	K-I									x	
AEVAC Inc 1500 Park Avenue South Plainfield, NJ 07080	P-I			x							x
AFRO-AM Inc 910 S. Michigan Avenue Chicago, IL 60605	Pr-I										x
Agency for Instructional Television Box A, 1111 W. 17th Street Bloomington, IN 47401	Pr-I	x	x	x	x		x			x	x
Allyn & Bacon Inc 470 Atlantic Avenue Boston, MA 02210	Pr-I		x	x	x		x			x	x
American Book Company 135 W. 50th Street New York, NY 10020	P-I			x				x			
American Educational Films 132 Lasky Drive Beverly Hills, CA 90212	Pr-I	x	x	x	x		x		x	x	x

Name & Address	Grade Range	Subject Areas									
		the arts	education	humanities	language arts/reading	library science/media	mathematics	music	physical education/sports	science	social sciences
American Library Color Slide Co Inc Box 5810, Grand Central Station New York, NY 10017	I	x								x	
American Map Co Inc 1926 Broadway New York, NY 10023	P-I	x		x						x	x
American Museum of Natural History Library-Photographic Collection Central Park W. at 79th Street New York, NY 10024	P-I	x								x	x
Paul S Amidon & Associates Inc 1966 Benson Avenue St. Paul, MN 55116	Pr-I		x		x		x			x	x
Aspect IV Educational Films Sub of Business Films Inc 41 Riverside Avenue Westport, CT 06880	P-I		x		x						x
Associated Educational Materials Co 14 Glenwood Avenue, Box 2087 Raleigh, NC 27602	Pr-I		x	x	x		x			x	
The Athletic Institute Inc 200 Castlewood Drive North Palm Beach, FL 33408	P-I		x						x		
Atlantis Productions Inc 850 Thousand Oaks Boulevard Thousand Oaks, CA 91360	P-I		x	x	x						x
Audio Book Company 14937 Ventura Boulevard Sherman Oaks, CA 91403	P-I		x		x						
Audio Visual Enterprises 911 Laguna Road Pasadena, CA 91105	Pr-I	x								x	x
Audio-Visual School Service 155 W. 72nd Street New York, NY 10023	P-I		x							x	x

Name & Address	Grade Range	Subject Areas									
		the arts	education	humanities	language arts/reading	library science/media	mathematics	music	physical education/sports	science	social sciences
Capitol Records Inc 1750 N. Vine Street Hollywood, CA 90028	Pr-I		x	x	x		x			x	x
Cellar Door Cinema Drawer P Osterville, MA 02655	P-I	x									
Center for Cassette Studies Inc 8110 Webb Avenue North Hollywood, CA 91605	I		x	x	x		x		x	x	x
The Center for Humanities Inc Communications Park Box 100 White Plains, NY 10602	P-I	x	x	x	x		x		x	x	x
Centron Educational Films 1621 W. Ninth Lawrence, KS 66044	Pr-I	x	x	x	x					x	x
Cereal Institute Inc 1111 Plaza Drive Schaumburg, IL 60195	Pr-I		x								
Children's Classics on Tape 6722 Bostwick Drive Springfield, VA 22151	P-I				x						x
Childrens Press 1224 W. Van Buren Chicago, IL 60607	Pr-I		x		x				x	x	x
Churchill Films 662 N. Robertson Boulevard Los Angeles, CA 90069	Pr-I	x	x		x		x	x	x	x	x
Cine'-Pic Hawaii 1847 Pacific Heights Road Honolulu, NI 96813	P-I		x		x		x		x	x	x
Civic Education Service 5420 27th Street, NW Washington, DC 20015	I										x

Name & Address	Grade Range	the arts	education	humanities	language arts/reading	library science/media	mathematics	music	physical education/sports	science	social sciences
William Claiborne 33 Union Square W. New York, NY 10003	P-I	x	x	x	x		x			x	x
Clarke Irwin & Co Ltd 791 St. Clair Avenue W. Toronto, ONtario M6C 1B8 Canada	P-I		x		x						x
Clarus Music Ltd 340 Bellevue Avenue Yonkers, NY 10703	Pr-I	x	x	x	x						x
Classroom World Productions Box 28166 Raleigh, NC 27611	Pr-I	x	x	x	x		x		x	x	x
Colonial Films 4315 ND Expressway Atlanta, GA 30341	P-I		x								
Communacad, The Communications Academy Box 541 Wilton, CT 06897	P-I				x						
Communications Group West 6606 Sunset Boulevard Hollywood, CA 90028	I		x		x					x	x
Comprenetics Inc 340 N. Camden Drive Beverly Hills, CA 90210	P-I	x	x		x						
David C Cook Publishing Company Public & Private School Division 850 N. Grove Street Elgin, IL 60120	Pr-I		x							x	x
Copymotion 1600 Broadway, Box 5173 New York, NY 10017	P-I	x			x		x				
Coronet Films 65 E. South Water Street Chicago, IL 60601	Pr-I	x	x	x	x		x			x	x

Name & Address	Grade Range	the arts	education	humanities	language arts/reading	library science/media	mathematics	music	physical education/sports	science	social sciences
Counselor Films Inc 146 Montgomery Avenue Bala Cynwyd, PA 19004	P-I	x	x	x	x				x	x	x
Counterpoint Films 14622 Lanark Street Panorama City, CA 91402	Pr-I		x	x	x						x
Creative Learning Inc 38 Nayatt Road Barrington, RI 02806	Pr-I	x	x		x			x		x	x
Creative Visuals Division/Gamco Industries Inc Box 1911 Big Springs, TX 79720	Pr-I		x	x	x			x			x
Crystal Productions 107 Pacific Avenue, Box 11480 Aspen, CO 81611	I	x	x		x				x	x	x
Current Affairs/Young World 24 Danbury Road Wilton, CT 06897	P-I	x	x	x	x				x	x	x
Cypress Publishing Corporation 1763 Gardena Avenue Glendale, CA 91204	Pr-I		x		x					x	x
Daughters of St Paul 50 St. Paul's Avenue Boston, MA 02130	Pr-I										x
Davco Publishers 8154 Ridgeway Skokie, IL 60076	I										x
Tom Davenport Films Pearlsone Delaplane, VA 22025	P-I	x			x	x					x
Murl Deusing Film Productions 1401 W. Hwy 50 Lot 163 Clermont, FL 32711	P-I									x	x

Name & Address	Grade Range	the arts	education	humanities	language arts/reading	library science/media	mathematics	music	physical education/sports	science	social sciences
Dimension Pictures 9000 W. Sunset Boulevard Los Angeles, CA 90069	Pr-I		x	x	x				x	x	x
Discovery Productions 151 E. 50th Street New York, NY 10022	I	x	x	x					x	x	x
Walt Disney Educational Media Co 500 S. Buena Vista Street Burbank, CA 91521	Pr-I		x	x	x		x			x	x
Donars Productions 407 N. Lincoln Avenue Loveland, CO 80537	P-I	x	x	x	x					x	x
Kevin Donovan Films Box 309 Glastonbury, CT 06033	I									x	x
Edplan Corporation Box 4361 Grand Central Station New York, NY 10017	Pr-I	x	x		x						x
Education Development Center 55 Chapel Street Newton, MA 02160	Pr-I		x							x	x
Educational Audio Visual Inc Pleasantville, NY 10570	P-I	x	x	x	x		x		x	x	x
Educational Communication Assoc 822 National Press Building Washington, DC 20045	P-I	x	x	x	x						x
Educational Design Inc 47 W. 13th Street New York, NY 10011	I		x	x	x					x	x
Educational Development Corporation 4235 S. Memorial Drive Tulsa, OK 74145	Pr-I		x		x		x			x	x

Name & Address	Grade Range	the arts	education	humanities	language arts/reading	library science/media	mathematics	music	physical education/sports	science	social sciences
Educational Dimensions Group Box 126 Stamford, CT 06904	P-I	x	x	x	x		x		x	x	x
Educational Direction Inc 181 Post Road Westport, CT 06880	P-I		x	x	x		x			x	x
Educational Enrichment Materials 357 Adams Street Bedford Hills, NY 10507	Pr-I	x		x	x		x			x	x
Educational Filmstrips 1401 1ᶜ h Street Huntsville, TX 77340	P-I	x	x	x	x		x		x	x	x
Educational Images Box 367 Lyons Falls, NY 13368	P-I	x								x	x
Educational Media Inc 115 E. Fourth Street Ellensburg, WA 98926	P-I						x		x		
Educational Research Inc 4021 Greenwood Road Shreveport, LA 71109	Pr-I		x		x		x				
Educational Technology Publications Inc 140 Sylvan Avenue Englewood Cliffs, NJ 07632	Pr-I		x								
Ed-Venture Films 1203 Isabel Street Burbank, CA 91506	P		x								
H M Edwards 1931 S. Newport Street Denver, CO 80224	Pr-I		x							x	
Herbert M Elkins Company 10331 Commerce Avenue Tujunga, CA 91042	P-I	x		x	x		x			x	x

Name & Address	Grade Range	the arts	education	humanities	language arts/reading	library science/media	mathematics	music	physical education/sports	science	social sciences
EMC Corporation 180 E. Sixth Street St. Paul, MN 55101	P-I		x	x	x		x		x	x	x
Encore Visual Education Inc 1235 S. Victory Boulevard Burbank, CA 91502	P-I	x	x	x	x					x	x
Encyclopedia Britannica Educational Corporation 425 N. Michigan Avenue Chicago, IL 60611	Pr-I	x	x	x	x		x		x	x	x
Enrich Inc 760 Kifer Road Sunnyvale, CA 94086	P-I				x		x		x		
Enrichment Materials Inc 50 W. 44th Street New York, NY 10036	Pr-I		x	x	x						x
Enrichment Reading Corporation of America 102 E. North Street, Iron Ridge, WI 53035	Pr-I				x		x			x	x
E S E Audiovisual 940 W. 22nd Street Hialeah, FL 33010	I	x	x							x	
Eye Gate Media Inc 146-01 Archer Avenue Jamaica, NY 11435	P-I	x	x	x	x		x		x	x	x
Fenwick Productions 134 Steele Road West Hartford, CT 06119	I			x							
The Fideler Company 31 Ottawa NW Grand Rapids, MI 49502	P-I										x
Film Communicators 11136 Weddington Street North Hollywood, CA 91601	Pr-I		x		x					x	x

Name & Address	Grade Range	the arts	education	humanities	language arts/reading	library science/media	mathematics	music	physical education/sports	science	social sciences
Film Modules Inc 172 Sullivan Street New York, NY 10012	P-I		x								
Filmfair Communications 10820 Ventura Boulevard Studio City, CA 91604	Pr-I	x	x	x	x		x		x	x	x
Films for the Humanities Inc Box 2053 Princeton, NJ 08540	I	x			x	x				x	x
Fine Arts Films Inc 11632 Ventura Boulevard Studio City, CA 91604	Pr-I	x	x							x	x
Fire Prevention through Films Inc Box 11 Newton Highlands, MA 02161	P-I		x								
Folkcraft Publishing Co Inc 10 Fenwick Street Newark, NJ 07114	Pr-I		x								
Folkways Recrods & Services Corp 43 W. 61st Street New York, NY 10023	P-I			x	x					x	x
Follett Publishing Company 1010 W. Washington Boulevard Chicago, IL 60607	Pr-I		x		x				x		x
Fordham Equipment & Publishing Co 3308 Edson Avenue Bronx, NY 10469	Pr-I	x	x	x	x		x		x	x	x
Franciscan Communications Center 1229 S. Santee Street Los Angeles, CA 90015	Pr-I		x	x							x
Friendship Press 475 Riverside Drive New York, NY 10027	P-I										x

Name & Address	Grade Range	the arts	education	humanities	language arts/reading	library science/media	mathematics	music	physical education/sports	science	social sciences
Frith Films Box 424 Carmel Valley, CA 93924	Pr-I				x						x
GAF Corporation 140 W. 51st Street New York, NY 10020	P-I	x	x	x	x		x			x	x
Girl Scouts of the USA 830 Third Avenue New York, NY 10022	P-I		x		x						x
Goldsmith's Music Shop Inc Audio Visual Department 301 E. Shore Road Great Neck, NY 11023	Pr-I				x					x	x
Graphic Curriculum Inc 699 Madison Avenue New York, NY 10021	P-I	x	x	x	x					x	x
Great American Film Factory Box 160281 Sacramento, CA 95816	P-I			x	x				x	x	x
Greenwood Press Inc 51 Riverside Avenue Westport, CT 06880	I										x
Grolier Educational Corporation Old Sherman Turnpike Danbury, CT 06816	Pr-I				x		x				x
Guidance Associates Inc 757 Third Avenue New York, NY 10011	K-I		x	x	x		x			x	x
Hammond Inc 515 Valley Street Maplewood, NJ 07040	Pr-I		x		x				x	x	x
Handel Film Corporation 8730 Sunset Boulevard Los Angeles, CA 90069	I	x	x	x						x	x

Name & Address	Grade Range	the arts	education	humanities	language arts/reading	library science/media	mathematics	music	physical education/sports	science	social sciences
Harcourt Brace Jovanovich Films 1001 Polk Street San Francisco, CA 94109	Pr-I	x	x	x	x		x			x	x
Harris County Center for the Retarded Inc Box 13403 Houston, TX 77019	Special Education										
Hayes Publishing Co Inc 6340 Hamilton Avenue Cincinnati, OH 45224	Pr-I		x								x
Hayes School Publishing Co Inc 321 Pennwood Avenue Wilkinsburg, PA 15221	Pr-I		x		x		x				x
D C Heath & Company 125 Spring Street Lexington, MA 02173	P-I				x		x			x	x
Stuart Hersh Productions 680 Fifth Avenue New York, NY 10019	Pr-I	x	x	x	x				x	x	x
Hester & Associates 11422 Hines Boulevard Dallas, TX 75229	Pr-I	x			x		x			x	
Alfred Higgins Productions 9100 Sunset Boulevard Los Angeles, CA 90069	K-I										x
Hoffman Electronics Corporation 4423 Arden Drive El Monte, CA 91734	P-I		x								
Holt, Rinehart & Winston School Department 383 Madison Avenue New York, NY 10017	Pr-I			x	x		x			x	x
Houghton Mifflin Company Media Department One Beacon Street Boston, MA 02107	Pr-I	x	x	x	x		x			x	x

Name & Address	Grade Range	the arts	education	humanities	language arts/reading	library science/media	mathematics	music	physical education/sports	science	social sciences
Hubbard Scientific Company Box 105 Northbrook, IL 60062	P-I		x						x	x	x
Hudson Photographic Industries Inc Irving-on-Hudson, NY 10533	Pr-P			x	x		x				x
Ideal School Supply Company 11000 S. Lavergne Avenue Oak Lawn, IL 60453	P-I				x		x				
Imperial Educational Resources 19 Marble Avenue Pleasantville, NY 10570	Pr-I	x	x	x	x		x		x	x	x
Imperial International Learning Box 548 Kankakee, IL 60901	Pr-I				x		x		x	x	x
Indian House Box 472 Taos, NM 87571	Pr-I										x
Instructional Aids Inc Box 191 Mankato, MN 56001	Pr-I		x						x	x	x
Instructional/Communications Technology Inc 10 Stepar Place Huntington Station, NY 11746	P-I				x						
Instructional Dynamics Inc 666 N. Lake Drive Chicago, IL 60611	P-I		x		x		x		x	x	x
Instructo/McGraw-Hill Paoli, PA 19301	Pr-I		x		x		x			x	x
Integrative Learning Systems Inc 140 N. Maryland Avenue Glendale, CA 91206	P-I		x		x						
Interculture Associates Box 277 Thompson, CT 06277	I	x	x	x	x						x

Name & Address	Grade Range	the arts	education	humanities	language arts/reading	library science/media	mathematics	music	physical education/sports	science	social sciences
International Film Bureau Inc 332 S. Michigan Avenue Chicago, IL 60604	Pr-I	x	x	x	x		x		x	x	x
International Film Foundations Inc 475 Fifth Avenue, Room 916 New York, NY 10017	I										x
International Motion Pictures Ltd Box 3201 Erie, PA 16512	I	x			x						x
Jabberwocky 4 Commercial Boulevard Novato, CA 94947	Pr-I				x		x				
January Productions Inc 124 Rea Avenue Hawthorne, NJ 07506	Pr-I		x				x		x		x
Joint Council on Economic Education 1212 Avenue of the Americas New York, NY 10036	P-I										x
Kauffman & Boyce Productions Box 283 Allston, MA 02134	P-I	x	x	x							x
Walter J Klein Co Ltd 6301 Carmel Road Charlotte, NC 28211	P-I		x								
Lawren Productions Inc Box 666 Mendocino, CA 95460	P-I	x	x								x
Learning Corporation of America 1350 Avenue of the Americas New York, NY 10019	P-I	x	x	x	x				x	x	x
Learning through Seeing Inc LTS Building, Box 368 Sunland, CA 91040	Pr-I		x		x			x			

Name & Address	Grade Range	Subject Areas	the arts	education	humanities	language arts/reading	library science/media	mathematics	music	physical education/sports	science	social sciences
Learning Tree Filmstrips 934 Pearl Street Boulder, CO 80302	Pr-I			x		x		x			x	x
Learning Ventures 666 Fifth Avenue New York, NY 10019	I			x	x	x						x
Peter Li Inc/Pflaum Press 2451 E. River Road Dayton, OH 45439	Pr-I			x								
Library Filmstrip Center 3033 Aloma Wichita, KS 67211	P-I		x	x	x	x		x			x	x
Library of Congress Recorded Sound Section, Music Division 10 First Street, SE Washington, DC 20540	Pr-I		x			x						x
J B Lippincott Educational Publishing Division East Washington Square Philadelphia, PA 19105	P-I					x					x	x
Listening Library Inc 1 Park Avenue Old Greenwich, CT 06870	Pr-I		x	x	x	x		x			x	x
The Little Red Filmhouse 666 N. Robertson Los Angeles, CA 90069	Pr-I		x	x		x						
Lohmann Films 1006 Sunset Court West Lafayette, IN 47906	P-I		x		x	x					x	x
Hubert A Lowman Route 1, Box 110 Arroyo Grande, CA 93420	P-I										x	x
Lyceum Productions Inc Box 1226 Laguna Beach, CA 92652	P-I				x	x					x	x

Name & Address	Grade Range	the arts	education	humanities	language arts/reading	library science/media	mathematics	music	physical education/sports	science	social sciences
Macmillan Films Inc 34 MacQuesten Parkway S. Mount Vernon, NY 10550	I	x	x	x	x		x		x	x	x
Marsh Film Enterprises Inc Box 8082 Shawnee Mission, KS 66208	Pr-I			x					x	x	x
Mast Development Company 2212 E. 12th Street Davenport, IA 52803	Pr-I				x		x		x		
McGraw-Hill Book Company 1221 Avenue of the Americas New York, NY 10020	Pr-I	x	x	x	x		x			x	x
Media Materials Inc Remington Avenue Baltimore, MD 21210	P-I		x		x		x			x	x
Media Research & Development Arizona State University Tempe, AZ 85281	P-I		x								
Media Research Associates Inc 1712 S.E. 23rd Street Salem, OR 97302	Pr-I		x					x			
Media Systems Inc 3637 E. 7800 S. Salt Lake City, UT 84121	I					x					
Memorex Corporation 1200 Memorex Drive Santa Clara, CA 95052	P-I		x								
Charles E Merrill Publishing 1300 Alum Creek Drive Columbus, OH 43216	Pr-I		x	x			x			x	x
Metropolitan Pittsburgh Public Broadcasting Inc 4802 Fifth Avenue Pittsburgh, PA 15213	Pr-I		x		x					x	

Name & Address	Grade Range	Subject Areas									
		the arts	education	humanities	language arts/reading	library science/media	mathematics	music	physical education/sports	science	social sciences
Micom Ltd 3405 W. Chester Pike Newtown Square, PA 19073	Pr-I	x	x	x	x		x		x	x	x
Midwest Visuals Inc Box 38 Brimson, MN 55602	I				x	x				x	x
Miller Productions Inc 800 West Avenue, Box 5584 Austin, TX 78763	Pr-I		x	x							
Milliken Publishing Company 1100 Research Boulevard St. Louis, MO 63132	Pr-I		x			x	x			x	x
Mini Productions Inc 725 Liberty Avenue Pittsburgh, PA 15222	P-I		x								
Arthur Mokin Productions Inc 17 W. 60th Street New York, NY 10023	Pr-I	x	x	x	x				x	x	x
Montage Films 924 Garden Street, Building G Santa Barbara, CA 93101	I				x	x				x	x
Moody Institute of Science 12000 E. Washington Boulevard Whittier, CA 90606	P-I						x			x	x
Moonlight Productions 2650 California Street Mountain View, CA 94040	I								x		
Mosaic Media Inc 413 Cottage Avenue Glen Ellyn, IL 60137	I						x				
Multi-Media Productions Inc Box 5097 Stanford, CA 94305	P-I		x			x	x			x	x

Name & Address	Grade Range	the arts	education	humanities	language arts/reading	library science/media	mathematics	music	physical education/sports	science	social sciences
Musilog Corporation Box 1199, 1600 Anacapa Santa Barbara, CA 93102	Pr-I	x									
National Career Consultants Inc 1300 E. Arapaho Road Richardson, TX 75081	I		x								
National Cathedral Association Washington Cathedral Mount St. Alban Washington, DC 20016	Pr-I	x	x								
National Dairy Council Division of Education 6300 N. River Road Rosemont, IL 60018	Pr-I									x	x
National Film Board of Canada 1251 Avenue of the Americas New York, NY 10020	Pr-I	x	x	x	x			x	x	x	x
National Geographic Society 17th & M Streets, NW Washington, DC 20036	P-I									x	x
National Livestock & Meat Board 444 N. Michigan Avenue Chicago, IL 60611	Pr-I										x
National Teaching Aids Inc 120 Fulton Avenue Garden City Park, NY 11040	I								x		
Nauman Films Inc Box 232 Custer, SD 57730	I	x	x	x					x		x
New Century Education Corporation 275 Old New Brunswick Road Piscataway, NJ 08854	P-I				x		x				
Noble & Noble Publishers Inc 1 Dag Hammarskjold Plaza New York, NY 10017	Pr-I		x		x						x

Name & Address	Grade Range	the arts	education	humanities	language arts/reading	library science/media	mathematics	music	physical education/sports	science	social sciences
Northwest Media Associates 158 Thomas Street Seattle, WA 98109	P-I		x	x	x						
Nystrom 3333 Elston Avenue Chicago, IL 60618	Pr-I		x							x	x
Olympus Publishing Company 1760 E. 1300 S. Salt Lake City, UT 84105	Pr-I	x	x								
Organization of American States Pan America Building 17th Street & Constitution Avenue Washington, DC 20006	Pr-I	x									
Outdoor Pictures Box 277 Anacortes, WA 98221	Pr-I	x	x	x	x		x			x	x
Pacific Records Company Box 26306 800 S. Fenton Street Denver, CO 80226	P-I				x						
Panoramic Teaching Aids Inc 1810 Rapids Avenue Alexandria, LA 71301	Pr-I				x		x			x	x
Paramount Communications 5451 Marathon Street Hollywood, CA 90038	Pr-I	x	x	x	x		x		x	x	x
Pathe News Inc/Pathe Pictures Inc 250 W. 57th Street New York, NY 10019	P-I		x	x					x		x
Pathescope Educational Media Inc 71 Weyman Avenue New Rochelle, NY 10802	Pr-I		x				x				x
Pathways of Sound Inc 102 Mt. Auburn Street Cambridge, MA 02138	Pr-I	x	x		x						

Name & Address	Grade Range	the arts	education	humanities	language arts/reading	library science/media	mathematics	music	physical education/sports	science	social sciences
Perkins School for the Blind Watertown, MA 02172	K-I Special Education		x								
Peter Pan Records 145 Komorn Street Newark, NJ 07105	Pr-K							x			
Pictura Films 111 Eighth Avenue New York, NY 10011	Pr-I	x	x	x	x		x				x
Pied Piper Production Box 320 Verdugo City, CA 91046	P-I				x		x				x
Pittaro Productions RD 1 Old Castle Point Road Wappingers Falls, NY 12590	P-I	x			x					x	
Playette Corporation 301 E. Shore Road Great Neck, NY 11023	Pr-I	x			x						x
The Plough Publishing House Rifton, NY 12471	Pr-I										x
Point Lobos Productions 20417 Califa Street Woodland Hills, CA 91367	I	x								x	x
Pomfret House Route 44 Pomfret Center, CT 06259	Pr-I				x	x			x	x	x
Portafilms Inc 4180 Dixie Highway Drayton Plains, MI 48020	P-I	x	x								x
Prentice-Hall Media Inc 150 White Plains Road Tarrytown, NY 10591	Pr-I	x	x	x	x		x			x	x

Name & Address	Grade Range	the arts	education	humanities	language arts/reading	library science/media	mathematics	music	physical education/sports	science	social sciences
Prentice-Hall of Canada Limited 1870 Birchmount Road Scarborough, Ontario M1P 2J7, Canada	Pr-I	x	x	x	x					x	x
Prothmann Associates Inc 650 Thomas Avenue Baldwin, NY 11510	I	x		x						x	x
Psythotechnics Inc 1900 Pickwick Avenue Glenview, IL 60025	Pr-I				x						
Pyramid Films 2801 Colorado, Box 1048 Santa Monica, CA 90406	I	x	x	x	x		x		x	x	x
Q-Ed Productions Inc 2282 Towns Gate Road Westlake Village, CA 91360	P-I		x		x		x			x	x
Ramsgate Films 704 Santa Monica Boulevard Santa Monica, CA 90401	Pr-I		x				x		x	x	x
Rand McNally & Company Box 7600 Chicago, IL 60680	Pr-I		x	x	x		x			x	x
Random House Miller-Brody Productions Inc 400 Hahn Road Westminster, MD 21157	Pr-I	x	x	x	x	x	x			x	x
RCA Music Service Educational Department 6550 E. 30th Street Indianapolis, IN 46291	P-I				x			x			
Recording for the Blind Inc 215 E. 28th Street New York, NY 10022	P-I	x	x	x	x		x			x	x
Regents Publishing Co Inc 2 Park Avenue New York, NY 10016	K-I				x						

Name & Address	Grade Range	the arts	education	humanities	language arts/reading	library science/media	mathematics	music	physical education/sports	science	social sciences
Rhythms Productions Whitney Building, Box 34485 Los Angeles, CA 90034	Pr-I		x					x			
RMI Media Productions Inc 120 W. 72nd Street Kansas City, MO 64114	Pr-I	x	x	x	x		x		x	x	x
ROA Films 1696 N. Astor Street Milwaukee, WI 53202	P-I		x	x	x				x		x
William H Sadlier Inc 11 Park Place New York, NY 10007	Pr-I		x								x
Sandler Institutional Films Inc Mel Road Hollywood, CA 90046	Pr-I		x		x						x
Alan Sands Productions 565 Fifth Avenue New York, NY 10017	P-I										x
S C Educational Television Commission 2712 Millwood Avenue Columbia, SC 29205	Pr-I	x	x	x	x					x	x
William Schlottmann Productions 536 E. Fifth Street, Suite 18 New York, NY 10009	P-I Special Education		x								
Scholar's Choice Ltd 50 Ballantyne Avenue Stratford, Ontario N5A 6T9, Canada	Pr-I	x			x				x	x	x
Scholastic Magazines Inc 50 W. 44th Street New York, NY 10036	Pr-I		x	x	x		x		x	x	x
Science & Mankind Inc Communications Park, Box 200 White Plains, NY 10602	P-I		x				x				

Name & Address	Grade Range	the arts	education	humanities	language arts/reading	library science/media	mathematics	music	physical education/sports	science	social sciences
Science Research Associates Inc 155 N. Wacker Drive Chicago, IL 60606	P-I	x	x	x	x		x	x	x	x	x
Science Software Systems Inc 11899 W. Pico Boulevard W. Los Angeles, CA 90064	P-I			x						x	
Screen Education Enterprises Inc Box C-19126 Seattle, WA 98109	Pr-I										x
Screenscope Inc 1022 Wilson Boulevard, Suite 2000 Arlington, VA 22209	P-I	x	x	x	x					x	x
Dale E Shaffer, Library Consultant 437 Jennings Avenue Salem, OH 44460	I		x	x	x						x
Shorewood Reproductions Inc 475 Tenth Avenue New York, NY 10018	I	x									
Silo Cinema Inc Box 7, Canal St. Station New York, NY 10013	I			x							x
Silver Burdett Company 250 James Street Morristown, NJ 07690	P-I			x	x		x			x	x
S-L Film Productions Box 41108 Los Angeles, CA 90041	Pr-I	x	x	x	x		x		x	x	x
Smithsonian Institution Office of Printing & Photographic Services Washington, DC 20560	P-I	x		x						x	x
Society for Visual Education Inc 1345 Diversey Parkway Chicago, IL 60614	Pr-I		x	x	x		x		x	x	x

Name & Address	Grade Range	the arts	education	humanities	language arts/reading	library science/media	mathematics	music	physical education/sports	science	social sciences
Soundings 2150 Concord Boulevard Concord, CA 94520	Pr-I	x	x	x	x						x
Spoken Arts Inc 310 North Avenue New Rochelle, NY 10801	Pr-I	x		x	x		x				
Spoken Language Services Inc Box 783 Ithaca, NY 14850	I				x						
Stanton Films 2417 Artesia Boulevard Redondo Beach, CA 90278	Pr-I				x				x	x	x
H M Stone Productions Inc 6 E. 45th Street New York, NY 10017	Pr-I	x	x	x	x		x			x	x
Sunburst Communications 39-41 Washington Avenue Pleasantville, NY 10570	I		x	x	x					x	x
Telekinetics 1229 S. Santee Street Los Angeles, CA 90015	Pr-I		x	x							x
Thorne Films Inc 934 Pearl Boulder, CO 80302	P-I									x	x
Time-Life Films Multimedia Division 100 Eisenhower Drive Paramus, NJ 07652	P-I	x	x	x	x		x		x	x	x
Troll Associates 320 Route 17 Mahwah, NJ 07430	Pr-I		x	x	x		x		x	x	x
Unitarian Universalist Association Department of Education & Social Concern 25 Beacon Street Boston, MA 02173	Pr-I		x		x						x

Name & Address	Grade Range	the arts	education	humanities	language arts/reading	library science/media	mathematics	music	physical education/sports	science	social sciences
United Church Press/Pilgrim Press 1505 Race Street Philadelphia, PA 19102	P-I		x								
United Learning 6633 W. Howard Street Niles, IL 60648	P-I		x	x	x		x			x	x
United Methodist Communications 1525 McGavock Street Nashville, TN 37203	Pr-I			x							x
United States History Society Inc 8154 Ridgeway Skokie, IL 60076	I										x
United Transparencies Inc Box 688 Binghamton, NY 13902	P-I		x	x	x		x			x	x
University of Missouri-Columbia 505 E. Stewart Road Columbia, MO 65211	Pr-I	x	x	x	x		x		x	x	x
US Committee for UNICEF 331 E. 38th Street New York, NY 10017	P-I										x
Vedo Films 85 Longview Road Port Washington, NY 11050	P-I				x				x		x
Viking Penguin Inc 625 Madison Avenue New York, NY 10022	Pr-I	x	x	x	x					x	x
Virginia State Department of Education Film Production Service, Box 6Q Richmond, VA 23216	P-I		x								x
Visual Education Corporation 14 Washington Road, Box 2321 Princeton, NJ 08540	P-I	x	x	x	x		x				x

Name & Address	Grade Range	the arts	education	humanities	language arts/reading	library science/media	mathematics	music	physical education/sports	science	social sciences
Visual Instruction Productions 295 W. Fourth Street New York, NY 10014	P-I		x						x	x	
Weber Costello 1900 N. Narragansett Chicago, IL 60639	Pr-I		x		x	x					x
Western Instruction Television Inc 1549 N. Vine Street Los Angeles, CA 90028	Pr-I				x					x	x
Weston Woods Studios Weston, CT 06883	Pr-P				x						
Westport Communications Group Inc 155 Post Road E. Westport, CT 06880	Pr-I	x	x	x	x		x		x	x	x
H Wilson Corporation 555 W. Taft Drive South Holland, IL 60473	P-I		x		x					x	x
Windmills Ltd Production Box 5300 Santa Monica, CA 90405	Pr-I		x	x	x						x
Xerox Education Publications/Xerox Films 245 Long Hill Road Middletown, CT 06457	P-I		x	x	x		x		x	x	x
Yellow Ball Workshop 62 Tarbell Avenue Lexington, MA 02173	P-I	x		x							x
Zia Cine Inc Anthropology Film Box 493 or 1626 Canyon Road Santa Fe, NM 87501	P	x	x	x						x	x

INDEX